The War on Mel Gibson

The War on Mel Gibson:
The Media vs. The Passion

Gary North

AMERICAN VISION
POWDER SPRINGS, GEORGIA

AMERICAN VISION

A BIBLICAL WORLDVIEW MINISTRY

THE MISSION OF AMERICAN VISION, INC. IS TO PUBLISH AND DISTRIBUTE BOOKS
THAT LEAD INDIVIDUALS TOWARD:

———

A personal faith in the one true God: Father, Son, and Holy Spirit

———

A lifestyle of practical discipleship

———

A worldview that is consistent with the Bible

———

An ability to apply the Bible to all of life

American Vision, Inc.

3150 Florence Road, Suite 2

Powder Springs, Georgia 30127-5385

www.americanvision.org

1-800-628-9460

———

Library of Congress Cataloging-in-Publication Data

North, Gary
   The War on Mel Gibson: / Gary North—1st ed.
   Includes bibliographical references and index.
   ISBN 0-915815-47-8 Softbound

This book is dedicated to

Mel Gibson

who has served as this
generation's Joseph of Arimathaea.

Contents

Preface
(TO BE READ)

MEL GIBSON HAS made a very large pile of money. Even before its release on DVD, *The Passion of the Christ* had grossed over $368 million at the box office in the United States, placing it as #7 in the history of American movies. Yet long before it opened, Hollywood and the liberal media were hopping mad. Millions of Protestants ignored the media and went to see a Catholic's movie. Some went twice.

What is going on? And why should you invest a day or two in reading this book to find out what I think is going on?

To help you decide, here is what I think is going on:

1. Gibson's movie presents the story of the atonement more clearly than in any previous mainstream movie.
2. This movie is an affront to liberal theology.
3. Gibson has hit a humanist nerve.
4. The movie was a box office blockbuster.
5. Liberal humanists recognize a threat to their continuing control over the media.
6. Christians see that they are not alone.

These factors have made *The Passion of the Christ* the most important recent event in the history of the American culture war. The Left went after Gibson and the movie early, but their efforts have backfired. The extent of that backfire is huge. It is possible—I believe highly probable—that this movie will mark a turning point in the culture war.

What do I mean by "culture war"? I mean a battle for the visible marks of supremacy in all of those areas of life that reflect the first principle of a society, but which are not bound by an oath. Three institutions are bound by an oath, implicit or explicit: the family, the church, and the state. In each of these institutions, there is an oath of allegiance. An oath is a promise. It is legally enforceable in a court of law, though not necessarily a civil court. There is a religious war going on inside each of these institutions, but I do not call this a culture war. I call it a covenantal war.

Culture is an extension of the cooperation of these three institutions. It encompasses the arts: music, painting, sculpture, and the graphic arts, including film. It encompasses the written word: literature and some forms of journalism. It encompasses food and all of the etiquette and ceremonies that accompany food. (If you think I'm wrong, invite your wife out to dinner, and then take her to a fast-food restaurant. Surprise!) Culture reflects and reinforces men's opinions on five crucial issues: God, man, law, causation, and time.

Culture surrounds modern man with a patchwork of competing visions and competing answers. The culture war exists because men do not agree on the answers to these questions.

> Who is God? What does He want mankind to do?
> What is man? To whom or what is mankind responsible?
> What are the rules governing men's life and death?
> What is the nature of historical cause and effect?
> Where are we headed? Where have we been?[1]

Culture is what we perceive when we cross some national borders but not others. When an American crosses into Canada, he does not perceive the change at first. His first indication is when he fills up his gas tank. The prices are different. There are no gallons; there are liters. But he has no problem mixing in culturally. He feels at home, or close to it. In contrast, when he crosses the border into Mexico, he senses the change immediately. It is not just the difference in language. He is in a different culture. He feels out of place. Eventually, he wants to go home. Home is where your culture is.

Let's get down to specifics. Why did Islamic terrorists target the twin towers? They tried to blow up one of them in 1993. They were successful in 2001. They could have selected another target. They didn't. What was it about destroying the twin towers that was worth dying for? These were not seats of government. They must have been symbolic. What did they symbolize?

They were the tallest buildings in the American city that is regarded as the center of world capitalism. Capitalism is transforming the world. Islamic radicals resent this. They wanted to make a statement. It was a statement without words. It was not a political statement. It was something else.

I would call it a religious statement. It was a religious statement regarding the vulnerability of capitalism. There is no indication that the terrorists were targeting banking or the stock market. Otherwise, they would have blown up a bank. So, what were they after? Symbols. Symbols of what? Symbols of a distinctly American civilization. They were making a statement against the culture of capitalism.

Inside the culture of capitalism, there is a war going on. Like the war that produced 9/11, this war has symbols. It also has tools. In some cases, the tools are the symbols. The television set is a symbol, but it is also a tool. The computer is a tool, but it is also a symbol. The yellow public school bus is a tool, but it is also a symbol.

The Passion of the Christ has become a symbol. It is my prayer and the humanists' nightmare that it is also a tool. This book is about *The Passion* as both a tool and a symbol. This book is a lengthy presentation of the battle over the film as a battle over its function as a symbol. But, underlying the debate, is the perception that it may become a tool.

Movies have long served as both symbols and tools. They reinforce people's opinions. The question is: Do they change people's opinions? Hollywood and the secular humanists who have been in control of this tool have always denied that it is a tool. "It's just entertainment." I think they knew better. Their overwhelmingly hostile reaction to *The Passion* indicates either that they always knew better or else they have now undergone a transformation in their thinking. I think it's the former. They always knew. The movies have been crowbars that Hollywood's humanists have used for a generation to pry Americans away from their first principles: religious, moral, and cultural.

I think it is time for Christians to recognize what has been done to them. It is also time for Christians to learn how to use this tool to fight back. We cannot all start a movie production company, but we can use the movies for our own cultural purposes, which are ultimately religious purposes. Mel Gibson has shown us the way. It can be done. Now the question is: Will it be done?

Is *The Passion* the first step in a systematic, comprehensive counterattack by Christians in a cultural war that Christians have been losing for almost a century? I think this is the case. So does Hollywood and Hollywood's cheerleaders in the media. This is why they are horrified.

In this book, you will get an idea of just how horrified they are, and also why.

This will cheer you up for the whole week. Maybe longer.

Notes

1. Ray R. Sutton, *That You May Prosper: Dominion By Covenant*, 2nd ed. (Tyler, Texas: Institute for Christian Economics, 1992). Available free at www.freebooks.com.

Part I

The War on Mel Gibson

Introduction

T HIS BOOK IS about a culture war that has been going on in the United States for well over a century. This war first became inescapably visible to the average American during what we call the Roaring Twenties: the era of Prohibition, the illegal speakeasy, and the flapper. It was also the era of the movies. Most people's knowledge of this period of American history comes mainly from television documentaries that rely heavily on extracts from movies of the era, either documentaries or commercial films. A few Americans may have read Frederick Lewis Allen's 1931 book, *Only Yesterday*, or some other historical study of the 1920s, but reading books is not the pathway to historical awareness for most Americans. Visual images are. The motion picture is modern man's most sophisticated aesthetic eye on the world. What it records, people are more likely to remember. They are likely to remember *The Passion*.

The Passion and Its Enemies

Mel Gibson's film, *The Passion of the Christ*, opened on February 25, 2004, a Wednesday. New movies generally open on Friday, in order to accommodate males who invite females for a date. Gibson had a reason for his selection of a mid-week date, one which had nothing to do with dating. February 25 was Ash Wednesday, the beginning of the Lenten season in Roman Catholicism. Only Good Friday would have been a more symbolic opening day.

The Passion is about Good Friday. No movie in history has ever recorded the horrors of the original Good Friday with greater emotional impact. Good Friday became visibly good only on the following Sunday.

When Jesus rose from the dead, the horror of Good Friday retroactively became the day of judgment: not for Jesus, as the authorities had imagined, but for Satan and his disciples, both demonic and human.

On Thursday, February 26, the *New York Times* ran an article by Sharon Waxman, "Will 'Passion' destroy a career?" It reported on what appeared to be a looming brick wall confronting Gibson.

> LOS ANGELES Mel Gibson's provocative new film, "The Passion of the Christ," is making some of Hollywood's most prominent executives uncomfortable in ways that may damage Gibson's career.
>
> Hollywood is a close-knit world, and friendships and social contacts are critical in the making of deals and the casting of movies. Many of Hollywood's most prominent figures are also Jewish. So with a furor arising around the film, along with Gibson's reluctance to distance himself from his father, who calls the Holocaust mostly fiction, it is no surprise that Hollywood—Jewish and non-Jewish—has been talking about little else, at least when it's not talking about the Oscars.
>
> Jeffrey Katzenberg and David Geffen, the principals of Dream-Works, have privately expressed anger over the film, said an executive close to the two men.
>
> The chairmen of two other major studios said they would avoid working with Gibson because of "The Passion of the Christ" and the star's remarks surrounding its release.

She quoted one of them as saying: "It doesn't matter what I say. It'll matter what I do. I will do something. I won't hire him. I won't support anything he's part of. Personally that's all I can do." In other words, the two men had launched a boycott, not merely against an offending product, which they could not control, but against the producer of that product. It was a boycott from the top. This is the most common boycott strategy by those in power who believe that they have a lock on a market. They can control supply by refusing to purchase the output of producers. Top-down boycotts are employed by elites. Bottom-up boycotts by final consumers are the boycotts of the people at the bottom of the economic hierarchy.

But would the boycott work? That all depended on the success of *The Passion*, according to John Lesher, an agent. "People here will work with the Antichrist if he'll put butts in seats." Then he made this observation about Gibson: "He put his own money where his mouth is. He invested in himself."[1] So, the crucial issue was this: Would Gibson get his money back, and then some?

By the time the article ran, Hollywood had the answer. The movie in its first day had grossed over $23 million in ticket sales. For investors to get their money back, a movie must make four times the investment. Gibson had invested between $25 million and $30 million, according to unofficial reports. By Sunday night—which was also Oscar night—*The Passion* had taken in $117 million. Every dollar after that would be pure gravy for Gibson: from new viewers, repeat viewers, foreign viewers, and DVD viewers—but not, we can be confident, network TV viewers. It will not be shown on network TV.

The day after the *New York Times* article appeared, the conservative newspaper, *Washington Times*, reported that the back-peddling had already begun in Hollywood. The fact that the movie had taken in over $23 million on its first day had caught the attention of the Hollywood's deal-doers. "Hollywood film company Dreamworks also backed away from remarks published in yesterday's New York Times suggesting that Hollywood producers will blacklist Mr. Gibson." Now, here is a verb to send chills down the spines of Hollywood liberals: *blacklist*. Blacklisting is what the industry did in the 1950s under pressure from the government and the anti-Communist public. That has been seen as the darkest era of the film industry by the post-1960 generation of film-makers. No one in Hollywood would call what these anonymous insiders were promising to do "blacklisting." They might call it something else. They just need a little more time to think about the correct term. Besides, now that the first day's receipts were in, "Let's forget about the whole thing."

A spokeswoman for Dreamworks founders Jeffrey Katzenberg and David Geffen released this statement:

"Neither one of us has seen the movie yet, and as such, we have not yet formed an opinion, but we respect Mel Gibson's rights as an artist to express his views," it said. "After all, this is America."

It is America, indeed—the nation, more than any nation in history, where money talks. Money does not just talk: it screams from the highest parapet.

Mark Joseph, an entertainment executive in Los Angeles and author of the upcoming book "The Passion of Mel Gibson: The Story Behind the Most Controversial Film in Hollywood History," said the film industry is in shock.

"This town is rocking," he said, "wondering what it all means. This is the film everyone deemed unreleasable."[2]

With respect to *The Passion*, to cite the French Revolution's most famous survivor, Talleyrand, Hollywood had done something worse than committing a crime. It had blundered.

The walls began tumbling down. It had not taken rams' horns to accomplish this. It had taken money—great wads of money. Millions of Americans had handed to Mel Gibson the tool of conquest in the free market economic system. And that was just the first day's receipts.

Within three weeks, Sharon Waxman, who had written the original article in the *New York Times*, "Will 'Passion' destroy a career?" wrote a follow-up story, "Hollywood Rethinking Films of Faith After 'Passion.'"

LOS ANGELES, March 14—As the overwhelming success of "The Passion of the Christ" reverberates through Hollywood, producers and studio executives are asking whether the movie industry has been neglecting large segments of the American audience eager for more openly religious fare.

Ah, the deal with "the Antichrist"—meaning Jesus Christ—already had willing takers.

> "You can't ignore those numbers," said Mark Johnson, a veteran film producer. "You can't say it's just a fluke. There's something to be read here."
>
> The movie's box-office success has been chewed over in studio staff meetings and at pricey watering holes all over Hollywood, echoed in interviews with numerous executives in the last week. In marketing departments the film is regarded as pure genius; its director, Mel Gibson, is credited with stoking a controversy that yanked the film from the margins of the culture to center stage, presenting it as a must-see. . . .
>
> Mr. Guber said that reaction to that movie's success was butting up against the feelings of many in Hollywood who dislike its widely criticized portrayal of Jewish responsibility in the death of Jesus.
>
> "There's both discomfort, amazement and anger—sometimes all at once," he said. "Greed and envy and anger and jealousy are all interesting bedfellows. They make for interesting conjugal visits in this town."
>
> Many movie executives said they were uncertain about whether to try to imitate "The Passion."
>
> "I wouldn't know how to duplicate this," said Jeff Robinov, the president of production at Warner Brothers.[3]

Behold, a man without guile! "I wouldn't know how to duplicate this." None of his peers do, either, but they will try. They will also lose money. In 1988, Hollywood had thought that *The Last Temptation of Christ* was a deeply religious film that would appeal to Christians. It was in fact a gob of spit in the eyes of God-fearing people, as I show in Chapter Eight. Hollywood, in areas theological, is economically blind.

> "It's not clear that Hollywood has the appetite or the attitude" to make religious movies, Mr. Guber said. Mr. Gibson's movie, he said, "in my judgment, has a politically religious point of view."
>
> "The question is: Is that a necessity for films of faith?"

Notice that he sees politics in the movie. The humanists' religion is the power religion. Anything that calls into question their religion, they see as political. The only political message in *The Passion* is this: don't trust the empire. Don't make Caesar your king. Humanists for over two centuries have built their faith in some version of salvation by politics. So, in this sense, Mr. Guber is correct: *The Passion* is deeply political.

A Turning Point

In this book, I argue that the release of *The Passion* is likely to become a watershed event, meaning a unique turning point in the direction in which American culture has been heading. By putting his own money on the line to finance his vision of the most important "career" in history, Mel Gibson revealed for all to see that what has sometimes been called the greatest story ever told still has avid listeners, and in this case, paying viewers. This story is the watershed of all watersheds in history. Furthermore, that part of the story which is presented by *The Passion* is the central fact of the story: Jesus of Nazareth was crucified and then rose from the dead. It was this event that confirmed what Jesus had said of Himself, namely, that He would rise from the dead on the third day. His bodily resurrection pointed to the truth of His other crucial affirmation, which He had affirmed publicly before the high priest. (Note: "son of the blessed" was in Jesus' day the equivalent to the phrase, "son of God.")

> And the high priest stood up in the midst, and asked Jesus, saying, Answerest thou nothing? what is it which these witness against thee? But he held his peace, and answered nothing. Again the high priest asked him, and said unto him, Art thou the Christ, the Son of the Blessed? And Jesus said, I am: and ye shall see the Son of man sitting on the right hand of power, and coming in the clouds of heaven. Then the high priest rent his clothes, and saith, What need we any further witnesses? Ye have heard the blasphemy: what think ye? And they all condemned him to be guilty of death (Mark 14:60–64).

Mel Gibson has reclaimed from theological liberals and skeptics the story of the death and resurrection of Christ. The media elite have steadfastly denied that the resurrection ever happened as the New Testament says it did. Gibson has brought to a generation of viewers that which the critics had been attempting to take away from them for well over a century, an effort that had escalated on-screen with a vengeance after 1959. Why 1959? It was in that year that *Ben-Hur* had become a smash hit at the box office. Lest we forget, that movie had a subtitle, as did the 1880 book: *Tale of the Christ.* The next year, it received eleven Academy Awards—the highest number ever granted until the feat was equalled *Titanic* and by the third installment *The Lord of the Rings*, a movie without nudity or illicit sex, which was based on the third volume of a trilogy written by a Roman Catholic scholar, who had honed his tale by reading it to a group of other Christian scholars called the Inklings. The Inklings' other famous member was C. S. Lewis, who was a member of the Church of England and the author of *Mere Christianity.*

In 1960, the year that *Ben-Hur* swept the Oscars, *Inherit the Wind* was released. The movie was loosely based on the 1925 Scopes' "monkey trial" in Dayton, Tennessee. The film, based on a play, viciously misrepresented the town, which had welcomed the outsiders with open arms. It also misrepresented the motivation of the townspeople. The trial had begun as a public relations stunt by the leaders of Dayton, who had wanted publicity and tourism, both of which the town soon got in abundance. The accused, a high school substitute biology teacher named John Scopes, was not even sure that he had taught anything about evolution on the day he was in class, which was why the defense never put him on the witness stand. He agreed to let the American Civil Liberties Union use him in its strategy to get the case to the U.S. Supreme Court after he was convicted. The ACLU's strategy was to lose the case. The late-arriving defense lawyer, Clarence Darrow, agreed with this strategy, which is why he ended his closing words by calling on the jury to convict Scopes, which it promptly did. The strategy backfired judicially when the Supreme Court refused to hear the case.[4] *Inherit the Wind* portrayed the town as bigoted, fundamentalist, and near-imbecilic. The movie was a frontal assault on the religious beliefs of tens of millions of Americans, something that the studio moguls of Hollywood had long avoided doing. As Sam Goldwyn had once said, "If you want to send a message, go see Western Union."[5] *Inherit the Wind* was a watershed. It sent America a message: the hands-off policy was about to end. Shortly thereafter, the on-screen groping began.

The film was a recapitulation of the strategy of the media elite in 1925. The news media in 1925 pilloried the fundamentalist Presbyterian lawyer for the prosecution, William Jennings Bryan, who had three times won the Democratic Party's nomination for President. Bryan was a far-left economic radical, but he was also an opponent of Darwinian evolution being taught in the public schools. He believed that Darwinism is heartless toward the less fit, meaning the poor. He cited Darwin verbatim to this effect.[6] As a radical reformer, he rejected the ethical implications of Darwinism. He was not a six-day creationist, as he admitted on the witness stand in Dayton, a scene which is portrayed accurately on-screen in *Inherit the Wind*. Beginning in 1921, he persuaded over half of the states to introduce laws prohibiting the teaching of Darwinism in the public schools, which is why the humanists had been working for four years to destroy him. When he volunteered to prosecute the case, an offer that local prosecuting attorneys could hardly turn down, the media sprang the trap. Hundreds of reporters came to Dayton from around the world. The trial was the first to be broadcast on national radio. Bryan won the case but lost the battle. He died in Dayton five days later.[7]

The trial's aftermath was more than anything the elite had dreamed of. In 1926, anti-conservatives in the Northern Baptist Convention and the Northern Presbyterian Church defeated the conservatives. Fundamentalism went into retreat on all fronts except one: church growth, which began to increase. No one in the media or the mainstream Protestant camp noticed this statistical fact until a generation later. In that same year, 1926, mainstream Protestantism's growth began to falter. In the 1960s, membership began to decline when deceased members were no longer replaced. But for half a century, fundamentalism went into its shell, from which it emerged, hesitatingly, in the Presidential election of

1976, and then aggressively in 1980, when fundamentalists and evangelicals elected Ronald Reagan.

American Church historians often date 1960 as the high water mark of mainstream Protestantism. It was Eisenhower's last full year as President. The man who had bankrolled liberal Protestantism for half a century, John D. Rockefeller, Jr., died. In that same year, Hollywood went on the offensive in the anti-Christian culture war with *Inherit the Wind*. In that same year, another studio released *Elmer Gantry*, a movie about a morally corrupt evangelist in the 1920s. It was based on Sinclair Lewis' 1927 novel. In both cases, Hollywood dredged up material that was a generation old. A year later, Burt Lancaster won an Oscar for his portrayal of Gantry. Yet the movie today is rarely seen on TV or rented. It was a period piece—for 1960 as well as 1927. I regard 1960 as a cultural turning point. Why? Because it was a religious turning point.

The Passion has now sent a message to Hollywood and the liberal media elite. Millions of Americans have had enough. They have demonstrated this at the ticket booth by validating Mel Gibson's vision in the way that counts in America: money. Within hours of the reports on the first day's ticket receipts, Hollywood began to back off, rather like Bela Lugosi's Dracula at the sight of a cross.

This book tells the story of how Christians have been in a culture war for almost a century. The arena is the darkened room of the movie theater. The battle for the control of the silver screen has become evermore crucial because the tax-funded public schools have failed to impart a level of literacy that was common in 1960. Television, music, and the movies have been the primary cultural battlegrounds for the hearts and minds of Americans for a generation. The Christians' counter-attacks have been poorly organized and unsuccessful so far.

Mel Gibson's triumph is therefore a unique event. It is the first financially successful Christian cultural counter-attack in the public square. Members of the Establishment media are hoping (but of course not praying) that *The Passion* will turn out to be a fluke, much as *Chariots of Fire* was in 1980. They want things to return to business as usual.

Things won't.

Mel Gibson is their worst nightmare. Movie buffs may remember Eddie Murphy's description in *48 Hours*, in which he plays a felon released from prison for two days in order to help a police officer track down a bad guy. Murphy is in a redneck bar. He utters his classic line: "I'm your worst nightmare: a nigger with a badge." Mel Gibson is Hollywood's worst nightmare: a Christian with a camera . . . and, from the look of the box office after two months, at least $100 million more than he started with.

Notes

1. Sharon Waxman, "New Film May Harm Gibson's Career," *New York Times* (Feb. 26, 2004). http://tinyurl.com/yvd05 Reprinted the next day in the *International Herald Tribune*. http://tinyurl.com/yvyp4

2. Julia Duin, "'Passion' critics retract reviews," *Washington Times* (Feb. 27, 2004). http://tinyurl.com/28p25

3. Sharon Waxman, "Hollywood Rethinking Faith Films After 'Passion,'" *New York Times* (March 15, 2004). http://tinyurl.com/yr3nk

4. Ray Ginger, *Six Days or Forever: Tennessee vs. John Thomas Scopes* (New York: Oxford University Press, 1958); Edward J. Larson, *Summer for the Gods: The Scopes Trial and America's Continuing Debate Over Science and Religion* (New York: Basic Books, 1997).

5. Cited by Michael Medved, *Hollywood vs. America: Popular Culture and the War on Traditional Values* (New York: HarperCollins, 1992), p. 307.

6. The offending passage appears in *The Descent of Man* (1871), Modern Library edition, p. 501. See Bryan, *In His Image* (New York: Revell, 1921), pp. 107–8.

7. Gary North, *Crossed Fingers: How the Liberals Captured the Presbyterian Church* (Tyler, Texas: Institute for Christian Economics, 1996), ch. 7. http://tinyurl.com/39j25

Is Being Pro-Christianity Anti-Semitic?

For I could wish that myself were accursed from Christ for my brethren, my kinsmen according to the flesh: Who are Israelites; to whom pertaineth the adoption, and the glory, and the covenants, and the giving of the law, and the service of God, and the promises; Whose are the fathers, and of whom as concerning the flesh Christ came, who is over all, God blessed for ever. Amen (Romans 9:3–5).

IN ALL OF Christian history, I know of nothing that matches this declaration of sacrifice. Jesus said—and Mel Gibson put on-screen—these words: "Greater love hath no man than this, that a man lay down his life for his friends" (John 15:13). But Paul went beyond these words to the more terrifying extent of laying down one's life: eternal death, meaning damnation. He said that he would be willing to do this on behalf of his kinsmen, the Jews. This came from a man who had not been treated well by his kinsmen. They had tried to kill him (Acts 23:16–21). When this attempt failed, they had falsely accused him in a civil court.

> And after five days Ananias the high priest descended with the elders, and with a certain orator named Tertullus, who informed the

governor against Paul. And when he was called forth, Tertullus began to accuse him, saying, Seeing that by thee we enjoy great quietness, and that very worthy deeds are done unto this nation by thy providence, We accept it always, and in all places, most noble Felix, with all thankfulness. Notwithstanding, that I be not further tedious unto thee, I pray thee that thou wouldest hear us of thy clemency a few words. For we have found this man a pestilent fellow, and a mover of sedition among all the Jews throughout the world, and a ringleader of the sect of the Nazarenes: Who also hath gone about to profane the temple: whom we took, and would have judged according to our law (Acts 24:1–6).

The problem here was not anti-Semitism on the part of Paul. The problem was anti-Christianity on the part of the Jews. Again, quoting Jesus:

But before all these, they shall lay their hands on you, and persecute you, delivering you up to the synagogues, and into prisons, being brought before kings and rulers for my name's sake (Luke 21:12).

"This Film May Arouse Anti-Semitism"

This has been the accusation that has caused the most controversy. The other one—that the film has too much violence—is not taken seriously by anyone who knows the history of R-rated on-screen violence, which rarely has anything to do with historical truth. If the critics are coming at this late date to protest on-screen violence, then they are either the products of a recent aesthetic conversion or else they have a not-very-well-hidden ideological agenda. The latter is more likely.

I have seen no reviewer argue that this film will arouse anti-Semitism in the United States, although there may be reviews out there that do say this. The common criticism is that this film will play in unnamed foreign countries. There, the reviewers tell us, this film will produce violence against Jews.

This is a curious argument. Who are these latent anti-Semites who are ready to bomb synagogues, or whatever? If they are not latent anti-

Semites, then why aren't they out there bombing synagogues today? The argument does not carry much weight.

To make this argument stick, the reviewers must identify two groups. One group is skinheads: Nazi emulators devoid of either a philosophy or a national leader. The other group is obvious: Muslims. There is no indication that acts of violence against Jews in Europe have been committed by anyone other than members of these two groups.

Why are skinheads going to attend *The Passion*? The rumor of violence, perhaps. But this violence is not committed by someone who is trying to get even with Jews. On the contrary, Jesus announces from the cross: "Father, forgive them; for they know not what they do" (Luke 23:34a). The call for forgiveness is added on-screen by the repentant thief, who asks the High Priest if he has understood what Jesus has just said. The hero of the movie calls on God to forgive His executioners. This does not do much to stir up the flames of revenge. To accept the movie is to abandon violence against the Jews in the name of Jesus.

Why will Muslims flock to the movie? To see the story of one of their prophets? Islam is monotheistic and unitarian. Jesus is said to be a prophet, but not the son of God. So, when the High Priest asks Jesus if He is the son of God ("the blessed" in the text), the Muslim will be no happier with Jesus' answer than the High Priest was.

> And Jesus said, I am: and ye shall see the Son of man sitting on the right
> hand of power, and coming in the clouds of heaven (Mark 14:62).

Why is this movie going to become the match that lights a fire of anti-Semitism? This, the reviewers do not make clear. But they do not let go of the accusation.

Abraham Foxman

The most vociferous promoter of this accusation is Abraham Foxman of the Anti-Defamation League (ADL), a Jewish pressure group that was founded in 1913. He did not publish a review in just one newspaper or magazine. He repeated his accusations in public for almost a

year, beginning with his open letter to Mel Gibson, which was released
to the media on March 24, 2003. By continually returning to the theme
of the movie's anti-Semitism, he set the tone for the hundreds of negative movie reviews that followed—reviews sometimes written by people
who had not seen the movie. In the orchestrated media attack that preceded *The Passion*, Mr. Foxman served as the orchestra's director. Here
are a few items taken from the ADL's Web site.

Press Release Anti-Semitism: USA
ADL Concerned Mel Gibson's 'Passion' Could Fuel Anti-Semitism if
Released in Present Form

New York, NY, August 11, 2003—After having attended a private
screening of Mel Gibson's new film, "The Passion," the Anti-Defamation League (ADL) today voiced concerns that the film, if released in
its present form, "could fuel hatred, bigotry and anti-Semitism" by reinforcing the notion of collective Jewish guilt for the death of Jesus.
An ADL representative was present at a private screening of "The Passion" at the Museum of Fine Arts in Houston, Texas.

"The film unambiguously portrays Jewish authorities and the Jewish mob as the ones responsible for the decision to crucify Jesus," said
Abraham H. Foxman, ADL National Director. "We are deeply concerned that the film, if released in its present form, could fuel the hatred, bigotry and anti-Semitism that many responsible churches have
worked hard to repudiate."

The version of Gibson's film, as previewed by Rabbi Eugene Korn,
ADL Director of Interfaith Affairs, contained a number of troubling
themes and images, all raising the specter of "deicide," or Jewish complicity in the death of Jesus.

"Sadly, the film contains many of the dangerous teachings that
Christians and Jews have worked for so many years to counter," said
Rabbi Korn. "This is not a disagreement between the Jews and Mr.
Gibson. Many theologically informed Catholics and Protestants have
expressed the same concerns regarding anti-Semitism, and that this

film may undermine Christian-Jewish dialogue and could turn back the clock on decades of positive progress in interfaith relations."[1]

This press release was a follow-up to another press release on August 4, in which Mr. Foxman complained that the film was being portrayed by its supporters as part of the culture wars. (I therefore predict that Mr. Foxman will not appreciate my book, but I think he will read it. He should. He needs to learn more about the culture war.)

> Discussions about Mel Gibson's forthcoming movie "The Passion" have taken a disturbing turn. Rather than focusing on an effort to find out whether Mr. Gibson is making a movie on the death of Jesus that is consistent with church teachings and free of the anti-Semitism that haunted passion dramas for centuries, the very raising of questions is now being depicted as a part of the culture wars that have overwhelmed American society in recent years. . . .

He raised two issues: (1) the possible inconsistency of the movie with church teachings, by which he meant Roman Catholic Church teachings after Vatican II (1962–65), and (2) the inapplicability of the negative category "culture wars" to Mr. Foxman's full-scale vendetta against *The Passion*. That is, Mr. Foxman threw two stones: (1) doubt regarding the moral integrity of Mel Gibson in writing, directing, and funding a theologically heretical movie, and (2) doubt regarding anyone, like myself, who suggests that this movie and its vociferous opponents—not to mention anonymous heads of studios who have threatened to boycott Mr. Gibson permanently—are part of a larger culture war. Then he went on:

> Why have we been raising questions as to whether Mr. Gibson's movie may be returning to outmoded, dangerous views of the Jewish role in the death of Jesus?
> First, because there has been a long history of the passion story i.e., the trials, crucifixion and resurrection of Jesus, being interpreted as holding the Jewish people responsible for killing Jesus. (*New York Sun*, Aug. 4, 2003)[2]

This statement indicated that in Mr. Foxman's data base of donors, there is apparently an audience of fearful Jews who really do worry about possible fall-out, to use an atomic age term, from a modern version of a medieval art form. Or could it be that he really does not believe this? If so, then why does he keep bringing it up? He wrote a letter to Mel Gibson privately, and then posted it on-line, so that donors and potential donors could read it.

ADL Letter to Mel Gibson
March 24, 2003

Dear Mr. Gibson

Based on initial media reports, we have serious concerns about the film you are currently making about the last hours of the life of Jesus, "The Passion," and would like to be assured that it will not give rise to the old canard of charging Jews with deicide and to anti-Semitism.

Passion plays have an infamous history of leading to hatred, violence and even death of Jews. Given your talent and celebrity, how you depict the death of Jesus will have widespread influence on people's ideas, attitudes and behavior towards Jews today.[3]

In another posting, we read:

ADL's concerns include:

The film portrays Jewish authorities and the Jewish "mob" as forcing the decision to torture and execute Jesus, thus assuming responsibility for the crucifixion.

The movie does this because the New Testament says that this is what happened. But Gibson succumbed to pressure and did not put English subtitles of the Aramaic words spoken in the film. Here is the New Testament's account:

When Pilate saw that he could prevail nothing, but that rather a tumult was made, he took water, and washed his hands before the multitude, saying, I am innocent of the blood of this just person: see ye to it. Then answered all the people, and said, His blood be on us, and on our children (Matthew 27:24–25).

So, the plain fact is this: Mr. Foxman was indirectly attacking the New Testament as being inaccurate. He used Mel Gibson as—sorry, I cannot resist—a whipping boy. Mr. Foxman continues:

The film relies on sinister medieval stereotypes, portraying Jews as blood-thirsty, sadistic and money-hungry enemies of God who lack compassion and humanity.[4]

Medieval stereotypes? Here, Mr. Foxman is not only grasping at stereotypical straws, he is also using inflammatory rhetoric at the expense of the truth. First, the movie portrays Jews at one point in history—the central point in history for Christians—as having condemned a supremely innocent man. So does the New Testament. This had nothing to do with blood-thirstiness. It had everything to do with trying to silence an opponent who was making a lot of trouble for the Jewish leaders. Second, the movie portrays only the Roman soldiers as being sadistic. It does portray some members of the Sanhedrin as beating Jesus. So do all four of the Gospels (Matt. 26:67; Mark 14:65; Luke 22:64; John 18:22). Third, the movie does not even hint of the possibility that Jews are money-hungry. It has only two scenes where money is involved, both involving the infamous 30 pieces of silver. The movie, like the New Testament, portrays Judas, not the Jews, as money-hungry. The New Testament is clear: Judas was a thief who controlled the disciples' money sack (John 12:6). He was in it for the money from day one. In the movie, the High Priest refuses to take back Judas' money. This scene is taken directly from the New Testament.

Then Judas, which had betrayeth him, when he saw that he was condemned, repented himself, and brought again the thirty pieces of silver to the chief priests and elders, Saying, I have sinned in that I have betrayed the innocent blood. And they said, What is that to us? see thou to that (Matthew 27:3–4).

Legally, Judas was a paid witness. This made void any testimony that he might offer in defense of Jesus. The Mishnah, the book of rabbinic law, clearly declares: "If a man takes payment for acting as a judge, his judgements are void; if for bearing witness his witness is void; . . . "[5] It was too late for him to testify on behalf of Jesus, either pro or con. When he offered to return the money, his offer was refused. The Sanhedrin was not interested in his money. It was interested in Jesus' conviction. Legally, the Sanhedrin could ignore Judas.

Here is the great irony. By his constant protesting, Mr. Foxman did more to gain publicity for *The Passion* than anyone except Mel Gibson. Mr. Foxman's laments were taken up by humanistic Jews and humanistic gentiles who wrote negative reviews of the film, in some cases before they saw it. Again and again in these reviews, we read of the anti-Semitism of this movie, yet almost always without an open admission that the movie sticks closely to the New Testament, except when it *softens* the condemnation of the Jews. For example, the movie depicts some Jews as opposing the absence of the Sanhedrin's quorum. No New Testament text suggests any such opposition. Also, these audible protests appear to have been dubbed after the film was shot. We cannot see anyone on-screen saying this.

When a reviewer of a movie that has yet to be released attacks it in print, he has received his information from someone. I think Mr. Foxman is the most likely candidate for being the primary source. Even if this is not the case, it will not hurt contributions to the ADL if his donors think it really is the case.

For the Sake of the Peace

Christians know that non-Christians do not believe the New Testament's account of the life of Christ. Some of these non-Christian critics are honest about their reason for rejection of the New Testament's historical details: they have a rival view of God, man, law, causation, and the future. Christians certainly understand why a practicing Jew does not accept the New Testament's account of the final hours of Jesus' pre-resurrection life. Furthermore, a practicing Jew knows that Christians know his position and the position of his peers. The questions Christians have for non-Christian film critics are these:

Is their criticism of this movie based on its artistic merits?

Is their criticism based on historical records that present an alternative view?

Is their criticism based on evidence that the movie will create anti-Semitic acts of violence?

Is their criticism of such a nature that it promotes peace between Christians and Jews?

Michael Medved

Michael Medved, an Orthodox Jew, says openly that he does not believe the gospel account. For years, he was a full-time movie reviewer for the PBS show, *Sneak Preview*. I have long trusted Medved's judgment on the quality of specific movies. He spent a dozen years reviewing movies every week. I never got the impression that he had a personal vendetta against any director. I also never saw him review a movie that he had not seen. In the language of a baseball umpire, he called them as he saw them. He established his credentials as a professional reviewer. I found from experience that I could trust his artistic judgment.

Medved has defended the artistic quality of *The Passion*.[6] As an Orthodox Jew, he did not defend its historical accuracy. But he did not challenge the movie just because the story is what the New Testament teaches.

For the record, let me make clear that I agree with Rabbi Boteach that the Christian scriptures provide an often unreliable, occasionally contradictory account of the persecution and execution of Jesus of Nazareth. If I believed that the Gospels represented an unfailingly accurate report of the events of two thousand years ago, I'd be a Christian, not a Jew. In defending Mel Gibson and his movie from hysterical and destructive charges of anti-Semitism, I have never suggested that the film portrays historical truth—any more than one must argue that popular Moses movies, from "The Ten Commandments" to "The Prince of Egypt," offer a precise and incontrovertible account of the Biblical story of the Exodus.

Does this sound reasonable, given Medved's personal religious confession? It does to me! Then he gets even more reasonable:

The only relevant question about "The Passion of the Christ" (which Rabbi Boteach acknowledges he hasn't even seen) is whether or not its portrayal of the last hours of Jesus falls within the mainstream of Christian interpretation and finds support within the Gospel text. The enthusiastic embrace of this movie by leaders of every Christian denomination, including the leading Catholic authorities, provides a definitive answer to that question and renders the specific attacks by Boteach largely irrelevant. In fact, all of the most controversial scenes and lines of dialogue stem directly from the Gospels, chapter and verse. This means that critics of the movie inevitably train their fire on Saints Matthew, Mark, Luke and John, rather than "Saint" Mel.

I could not have said it better myself. In fact, I could not have said it as well. He then raises the issue of maintaining good relations between Christians and Jews.

Of course, Jewish observers retain a perfect right to challenge sacred Christian texts, or to denounce the altogether conventional interpretation of those texts by a major filmmaker, but one might reasonably inquire what possible purpose such arguments can serve? By what right do Rabbi Boteach and his many outspoken allies in the Jewish community demand that Mel Gibson and his innumerable supporters among Protestant and Catholic clergy should reject their own religious tradition to accept a Jewish version of the death of their savior? After many centuries of Christian persecution of Jews, we have finally won the unquestioned right to reject the Gospel claims, and yet live in peace with our gentile neighbors. But this precious right to deny the accuracy of New Testament texts does not somehow empower us to insist that our Christian fellow citizens must join us in that denial.

This gets to the heart of the matter. The attacks on the film are frequently attacks on the moral right of Christians to tell on-screen the central story of their faith. Of course, no critic in the United States is so foolish as to attack the *legal* right of Christians to tell this story. Americans would reject such an implication as undermining religious liberty. But the critics' implication is that we Christians have a *moral* obligation not to tell this story our way, because our theological opponents disagree with our version.

> For reasons that defy rational explanation, Rabbi Boteach insists upon picking an ugly public fight with believing Christians who view their own sacred books in the same way the Rabbi views the Torah—as the inerrant word of God. To characterize elements of the Gospels as "fabrications" and "cheap frauds," as Boteach does in one of his columns, hardly helps the cause of Jewish-Christian cooperation.[7]

Medved is here invoking an old rule of rabbinical law: "for the sake of the peace." Jewish legal historian George Horowitz has explained this principle.

> Halakot [law] and customs which discriminated against Gentiles and which might, therefore, be enforced or practiced through perhaps "legally" valid, because it might reflect unfavorably on the Jewish people, its moral and its religion. "For the Sake of the Peace" was in effect an equitable principle which modified the strict law, with respect to treatment of Gentiles.[8]

Horowitz cites the Talmud in this instance:

> "For the sake of the peace," one should greet pagans even on their religious festivals though it may seem like honoring their idols (*M. Shev`it* IV, 3 and commentaries).[9]

Medved tried to head off the controversy. He phoned Mr. Foxman and invited him to appear on his radio show. He was turned down—more than once, according to Medved.[10] Then he exposes the treatment that Gibson received from the ADL.

> On August 8, Gibson and his associates traveled to Houston for a special screening of his still unfinished motion picture. More than 30 members of the Jewish community had been invited to the showing and subsequent discussion, along with 50 evangelical and Catholic leaders. Rabbi Eugene Korn, director of interfaith affairs for the ADL (he has since resigned from the organization), signed a confidentiality agreement, as did other members of the audience, promising not to discuss what he had seen. This pledge did not prevent the rabbi from telling The Jewish Week within hours of the screening that the movie "portrays Jews in the worst way as the sinister enemies of God."

This answers the accusation, often repeated, that Gibson showed the movie only to Christians. He initially wanted to cooperate with the Jewish community. He received no cooperation.

> In more than a half dozen conversations with Gibson, I heard him express his passionate desire to avoid hurting the Jewish community or its members. He consistently declares that he always wanted his movie to unite people rather than divide them. Before the setback in Houston, Icon had announced plans for a "Jewish initiative" and had begun assembling lists of Jewish opinion leaders to respond to the film and to help shape study guides and educational materials to be distributed along with it. Those plans are now on hold because of Icon's sense of betrayal following the public relations disaster in Houston.

Medved is correct: the attack by the ADL was self-defeating. It could not achieve its stated goals.

What did the ADL and its allies hope to accomplish with such bitter denunciations? The public condemnation of Gibson's movie made it less likely that he would re-edit the film to avoid offending the Jewish community. Given Gibson's often-expressed lofty intentions for his cinematic labor of love, how could he be seen as compromising his own vision of biblical truth for the sake of mollifying organizations and individuals who had already cried wolf over his alleged bigotry? Any perceived public surrender by Gibson to angry pressure from Jewish organizations would have thrown the integrity of his project into question.[11]

Medved also understood this inescapable fact: "If the film becomes a hit, the overwrought Jewish critics of the film will have succeeded only in demonstrating their irrelevance."

Daniel Lapin

Medved's rabbi, Daniel Lapin, understands how high the stakes in this dispute are for observant Jews who live in the United States. He warned in the fall of 2003 that the film's critics were jumping the gun. They had not seen the film.

Never has a film aroused such hostile passion so long prior to its release as has Mel Gibson's Passion. Many American Jews are alarmed by reports of what they view as potentially anti-Semitic content in this movie about the death of Jesus, which is due to be released during 2004. Clearly the crucifixion of Jesus is a sensitive topic, but prominent Christians who previewed it, including good friends like James Dobson and Michael Novak who have always demonstrated acute sensitivity to Jewish concerns, see it as a religiously inspiring movie, and refute charges that it is anti-Semitic. While most Jews are wisely waiting to see the film before responding, others are either prema-

turely condemning a movie they have yet to see or violating the confi-
dentiality agreements they signed with Icon Productions.

But he did not limit his criticism to the pre-release and therefore
premature attacks on the film.

> I believe those who publicly protest Mel Gibson's film lack moral
> legitimacy. What is more, I believe their actions are not only wrong
> but even recklessly ill-advised and shockingly imprudent. I address
> myself to all my fellow Jews when I say that your interests are not be-
> ing served by many of those organizations and self appointed defend-
> ers who claim to be acting on your behalf. Just ask yourself who most
> jeopardizes Jewish safety today, Moslems or Christians?

This was a response to Abraham Foxman and the ADL, surely, and
to those who dutifully followed his lead. He then referred to the movie, more than any movie, which attacked Christianity and aroused the
Christian community: *The Last Temptation of Christ*.[12] Jews did not
come to Christians' defense, he reminded his readers.

> You may also remember Martin Scorsese's 1988 film The Last
> Temptation of Christ. Then too almost every Christian denomination
> protested Universal's release of a movie so slanderous that had it been
> made about Moses, or say, Martin Luther King Junior, it would have
> provoked howls of anger from the entire country. As it was, Christians
> were left to defend their faith quite alone other than for one solitary
> courageous Jew, Dennis Prager. Most Americans knew that Universal
> was run by Lew Wasserman. Most Americans also knew Lew's ethnic-
> ity. Perhaps many now wonder why Mel Gibson is not entitled to the
> same artistic freedom we accorded Lew Wasserman?

He then went after the accusation, repeated over and over, that the
movie is dangerous because passion plays in medieval times led to attacks on Jews. Why bring this up today, especially in the United States?

In truth however, even though Catholics did kill Jews in Europe, I do not believe that the often sad history of Jews in Europe is relevant now. Why not? Because in Europe, Catholic church officials wielded a rapacious combination of ecclesiastical and political power with which they frequently incited illiterate mobs to acts of anti-Jewish violence. In America, no clergyman secures political power along with his ordination certificate, and in America, if there are illiterate and dangerous thugs, Christianity is a cure not the cause. In America, few Jews have ever been murdered, mugged, robbed, or raped by Christians returning home from church on Sunday morning. America is history's most philo-Semitic country, providing the most hospitable home for Jews in the past two thousand years. Suggesting equivalency between American Christians today and those of European history is to be offensive and ungrateful. Quite frankly, if it is appropriate to blame today's American Christians for the sins of past Europeans, why isn't it okay to blame today's Jews for things that our ancestors may have done? Clearly both are wrong and doing so harms our relationships with one of the few groups still friendly toward us today. Jewish groups that fracture friendship between Christians and Jews are performing no valuable service to American Jews.

Then there is the issue of selective criticism. Criticism should not be based on who stands to profit from a movie. But this has been the case. He raised the issue of *The Gospel of John*.

Again, why would the soon to be released new movie, The Gospel of John, be utterly immune to the censoring tactics of certain Jewish organizations? After all, the soundtrack includes virtually every word of the Gospel including the most unflattering descriptions of Jewish priests and Pharisees of Jesus' time, along with implications of their complicity in the Crucifixion, yet not a peep of Jewish organizational protest. Could their conspicuous silence possibly have anything to do with the ethnicity of the producers of The Gospel of John? These include Garth Drabinsky, Sandy Pearl, Joel Michaels, Myron Gottleib, and Martin Katz. So if Jews quote the Gospel it is art but if Mel Gibson does the same, it is anti-Semitism? The Talmudic distinction eludes me. It probably eludes most Christians too.

Finally, he raised the issue that Medved also raised: *for the sake of the peace.*

> Finally I believe the attacks on Mel Gibson are a mistake because while they may be in the interests of Jewish organizations who raise money with the specter of anti-Semitism, and while they may be in the interests of Jewish journalists at the New York Times and elsewhere who are trying to boost their careers, they are most decidedly not in the interests of most American Jews who go about their daily lives in comfortable harmony with their Christian fellow citizens. You see, many Christians see all this as attacks not just on Mel Gibson alone or as mere critiques of a movie, but with some justification in my view, they see them as attacks against all Christians. This is not so different from the way most people react to attack. We Jews usually feel that we have all been attacked even when only a few of us suffer assault on account of our faith.[13]

Undermining the Peace

These two Orthodox Jews, who are therefore self-consciously in the tradition of the Pharisees, understand that the age-old conflict between their tradition and the Christian tradition has been marked by illegiti-mate actions on both sides. In our day, peace has been restored in the West, with the exception of Islamic protests against a tiny number of Jews in Europe. In the United States, such actions have been limited to economic and social discrimination by Christians prior to 1945, and by the "good old boys network" among those Jews who favor each other in economic dealings—a matter of voluntary, non-coercive liberty. This network is more visible in Hollywood than anywhere else. These men see that the attacks on *The Passion* as an anti-Semitic movie rests on an assumption: criticism of the Sanhedrin that condemned Jesus is the equivalent of criticism of peaceful Jews who live among us. In a time when there has never been greater peace between Jews and Christians, they ask: Why wave the flag of anti-Semitism against a movie which does for Christians what movies on Old Testament figures do for Jews? Why shouldn't Christians be allowed to fund their own films and offer to sell tickets to the public without being verbally tarred and feathered for putting on a screen what their central religious texts say took place?

For the sake of the peace on both sides, Gibson should have been left in peace by Jewish detractors. Besides, if this had happened, the film might not have done much better at the box office than *The Gospel of John*. The critics created a level of "buzz" that the producers of *The Gospel of John* would have paid millions for. The critics did this free of charge.

The Legion of Decency in 1934 had the wisdom not to tell anyone that its survey revealed that its ban would probably raise a movie's ticket sales. Will Hays and Joe Breen thought it was better to work behind the scenes with movie producers who thought they had a lot of clout with the audience. In "plain site", for all the world to see, Abraham Foxman and his peers have revealed to the world what everyone in Hollywood should have known from day one: *controversy sells tickets*.

This controversy was unnecessary. One of my goals for this book is to deflect the accusation that this controversy is a matter of Judaism vs. Christianity. What this controversy is about is what Mr. Foxman explicitly denied: the culture war. Mr. Foxman and his gentile allies share a common vision and a common theology. It has a creed: "There is, at the most, one God." Neither Rabbi Lapin nor I proclaims this creed.

Let practicing Jews and practicing Christians continue to defend the authority of our rival texts. Let humanistic Jews and humanistic gentiles keep out of it. But they cannot bring themselves to keep out of it. They understand, just as we "authoritative text" people understand, that the larger conflict is the kingdom of man vs. the kingdom of God, moral and cultural relativism vs. a God who judges in history and eternity. This is a war of the worldviews: rival views of God, man, law, judgment, and the future. It is one of history's ironies that the self-proclaimed relativists, through their authoritarian attacks on the texts and all those who believe in them, have driven old enemies into a corner, where we now prefer to shoot outward rather than inward.

Patterson's Forthright Admission

One author was willing to say what the movie's critics have generally been unwilling to admit: their target is the New Testament. In an article published in *The Jewish Press* and reprinted widely on the Web, Charles Patterson announced the following.

> The trouble with Mel Gibson's film "The Passion" that opens in more than 2000 movie theaters on Ash Wednesday (Feb. 25) is not the film itself, but the gospel story on which its based. The gospel story, which has generated more anti-Semitism than the sum total of all the other anti-Semitic writings ever written, created the climate in Christian Europe that led to the Holocaust. Long before the rise of Adolf Hitler the gospel story about the life and death of Jesus had poisoned the bloodstream of European civilization.

His article is titled "A Whiff of Auschwitz: Mel Gibson and the Gospel of Anti-Semitism." Dr. Patterson is obviously not one to pussyfoot around.

> Can anything at all be learned from seeing this 21st century cinematic Passion play? Well, should historical curiosity compel you to want to see the gospel story fleshed out in living color while at the same time providing you with a whiff of the world it created—the Crusades, Inquisition, Oberammergau, and ultimately Auschwitz—a word of caution is in order: if you ordinarily wear a yarmulke, don a baseball cap instead.[14]

If Gibson's other critics were equally forthright, their readers would more readily recognize the critics' hidden agenda. This would make the critics appear in a different light from that of faithful defenders of the arts against a man who has misused art to unleash anti-Semitism. Rather than attacking Gibson, they would openly attack the New Testament and Christianity. But that would not suit their agenda, which is to fool naive gentiles into believing that Gibson, the sinister director, rather than Christianity is their target. I am not speaking merely, or even mainly, of Gibson's Jewish critics. I am speaking of the humanistic Establishment in general. But, from what I have read of their rants—and I have read too much—they take their rhetorical cues from Mr. Foxman, while harboring a resentment of the New Testament, as manifested by Dr. Patterson.

Prof. Goldhagen's Equally Hostile Attack

Here, a famous scholar logs in. Harvard University's Daniel Goldhagen is the author of *A Moral Reckoning: The Role of the Catholic Church in the Holocaust and Its Unfulfilled Duty of Repair* (2003) and *Hitler's Willing Executioners: Ordinary Germans and the Holocaust* (1997). His article appears in the Jewish magazine, *Forward*, which is also available in Yiddish and Russian. As you can imagine, he does not like *The Passion*. First, he hates Catholicism's crucifix.

> I have often thought but kept to myself what a gruesome thing they are, traditional crucifixes, each one with the likeness of a mangled, agonized body affixed cruelly to it. I sometimes wondered, even as a child, what kind of a religion would want children to look at an image of a suffering, dying or dead man, with nails piercing his hands. What is its effect upon them? Why would the spiritual leaders of any religion want their flock to gaze regularly at such horror, to gaze lovingly at such horror, to feel exalted at the image of such horror?

Second, he thinks that the symbol of a man on a cross is perverse.

> The aestheticizing, indeed fetishizing, of violence and horror is at the core of the crucified Jesus as an icon and symbol, and it clings allusively to even the visually tamer cross.

Given his view of the crucifix as "fetishizing" violence and horror, it is understandable why he would not enjoy the on-screen story of Jesus on the road to His death. He joins the chorus of the outraged. It is rare that a Harvard professor gets this excited about anything, other than not being granted tenure. He pulls no punches.

> Gibson's film takes the fetishizing of horror and death that exists within Christianity to some sort of sickly logical conclusion. Visually, iconographically and symbolically, Gibson's "Passion" is a sadomasochistic, orgiastic display that demonizes Jews as it degrades those who revel in viewing the horror. His movie's emotional and literal climax centers on an excruciatingly long, slow-motion, graphic depiction of the entire process of crucifixion. Its orgy of unsurpassed and virtually unremitting sadism restores this part of the Jesus story—de-emphasized by the Catholic Church since the Vatican II reforms—to center stage, to haunt all those who would follow Jesus with indelible, iconic images of cruelty. Gibson has thus unwittingly exposed the misguidedness of this cult of death. To the extent that such a vision of God dominates and obscures Jesus' Christian ministry of life, love and good works (as it does almost totally in the film), Gibson has also unveiled its meanness.

Sadomasochist? That is someone who delights in pain. This was not Jesus. Orgiastic? That is sexual debauchery. This was not Jesus. Orgy of unremiting sadism? That sounds like Roman soldiers to me. Cult of death? That is Christianity, of course.

He asks: Where are love and good works? Theological liberals want only love and good works, except when dealing with Nazism—the only absolutely evil thing in the ethical relativist's worldview. As for judgment, especially God's, they want none of it. This is why Gibson's film has outraged them. It shows them the depths to which men can sink. It makes brutality by the state seem—horror of horrors—brutal!

In his review, he of course praises theologically liberal Christians, as well he should, for they share his theology: "There is, at the most, one

God." They also share his cultural prejudices. So, Gibson and all that he represents—you and me—draw his ire and his fire.

> He restores a blood-drenched Christian cult of death in all its horror, terror and visual violence, with (a misogynist's) Satan and her bloodthirsty Jewish minions—the assembled mass of Jews led by their authoritative religious leaders speaking for Judaism—chanting "Crucify him! Crucify him!" Gibson labors to restore the Jews to their central medieval roles as the fearsome, corporeal opponents of good and of God.

What enrages the good professor more than anything else is that Gibson has access to a camera, and he knows how to use it.

> If all this had remained Gibson's private obsession, it would be merely pathetic. But Gibson has used a grotesquely manipulative Hollywood film—with the potential to reach billions—to take public vengeance. At the dawn of the third millennium, he has thrown the gauntlet down before the more progressive versions of Christianity and spread this medieval vision to the vast Catholic and Christian world that is less progressive and more susceptible to it. At the same time, in an indelible medium of unparalleled visual power and homiletic reach, he has renewed the most heinous calumny of the first two millennia, that the Jews are guilty in the murder of God.[15]

Today, Gibson has a lot more than a camera. He has a fortune. He also has millions of followers who are now personally committed to him because he made *The Passion*, and the whole world knows it. This no doubt upsets Prof. Goldhagen even more than he was when he wrote his review.

Hillary Clinton's Favorite Rabbi Piles On

Rabbi Michael Lerner is the head of the Tikkun Community, which is described as "an interfaith peace and justice organization." I can believe it. His book, *The Politics of Meaning*, was made famous by Hillary Clinton, who used the phrase in a 1993 speech defending her proposed socialized medicine program, which Congress promptly voted down.[16] Her speech was published in Tikkun's magazine, which has the appropriate title, *Tikkun*.[17] On March 31, 2004, *The International Herald Tribune* ran his article, "Mel Gibson revives an old message of hate..." Here, we learn the following.

> Mel Gibson unlocked the secret of why Americans have never confronted anti-Semitism in the way that we did with the other great systems of hatred (racism, sexism, homophobia) when he told an American TV audience in February that "the Jews' real complaint isn't with my film ('The Passion of the Christ') but with the Gospels."

I have done my best in this chapter to show why Gibson's accusation is on-target. This is exactly why certain Jews have gone on the attack, and continue to attack the film. Rabbi Lerner immediately confirms Gibson's accusation by attacking the factual integrity of the New Testament. He suggests that the writers of the Gospels sought to blame Jews rather than Rome for the crucifixion. This is a common accusation by Jews who are critical of the movie and the New Testament.

> The Gospels were written, many historians tell us, some 50 years after Jesus' death at a time when early Christians (most of whom considered themselves Jewish) were engaged in a fierce competition with a newly emerging rabbinic Judaism to win the hearts and minds of their fellow Jews and the minds of the disaffected masses of the Roman empire.
>
> The Gospels sought to play down the antagonism that Jews of Jesus' time felt toward Rome, so they displaced the anger at his crucifixion instead onto those Jews who remembered Jesus as an inspiring and revolutionary teacher (not a Messiah, not God).

I ask: If the Gospels were written half a century after the death of Jesus—a highly speculative thesis that is difficult to prove[18]—how many Jews were still alive "who remembered Jesus as an inspiring and revolutionary teacher (not a messiah, not God)"? Any Jew by that late date who thought Jesus was an insprired teacher, yet neither the Messiah nor God, was a member of one of the smallest identifiable religious groups in the Roman world. This would have been a decade after the fall of Jerusalem and the fall of Massada. By that time, church growth was taking place mainly in the gentile world. Why would gentiles have cared one way or the other about a tiny subset of Jews who regarded Jesus as an inspired teacher, but neither the Messiah nor God? Also, why would the Gospels' writers have written accounts in which Jesus claimed to be both the Messiah and God—claims which, unless true, were marks of a self-deluded madman rather than an inspired teacher? All of this escapes Rabbi Lerner.

> The result: an account that portrays Jews as willfully calling on the Romans to kill Jesus, rejecting the supposed compassion of the Romans, and thereby earning the hatred of humanity for the Jews' supposed collective responsibility for this act of deicide. Conversely, Jesus' Judaism, his viewing the world through the frame of his Jewish spiritual practice and Torah-based thinking, is played down or at times completely obscured.

I see: the accounts did not portray Jesus as a Torah-based thinker. Well, except maybe for this teensy-weensy exception:

> Think not that I am come to destroy the law, or the prophets: I am not come to destroy, but to fulfil. For verily I say unto you, Till heaven and earth pass, one jot or one tittle shall in no wise pass from the law, till all be fulfilled. Whosoever therefore shall break one of these least commandments, and shall teach men so, he shall be called the least in the kingdom of heaven: but whosoever shall do and teach them, the same shall be called great in the kingdom of heaven (Matthew 5:17–19).

Then Lerner waves the bloody swastika to scare away defenders of the film.

> In the aftermath of World War II, many principled Christians recognized that the Holocaust was possible in part because Hitler was able to draw upon the cultural legacy of hatred toward Jews nurtured by this kind of Christian teaching. The Catholic Church and some Protestant denominations have sought to distance themselves from this long history of demeaning the Jews. But only a few Christians were willing to take responsibility for the devastating impact of the hateful representations of Jews that suffused the Gospels.

If this is not an attempt to send Gibson and the movie's fans up guilt creek without a paddle, I wonder what would be.

Lerner heaps praise, as do many of Gibson's critics, on theological liberals and modernists (progressives), who have openly abandoned the New Testament and its teachings. These liberals share the same humanist faith, so they act as reinforcing chorsuses for each other. But Lerner says that even they have had a blind spot: the evil social effects of the story of the crucifixion.

> Liberals and progressives in the late 20th century did an impressive job of confronting and educating the public about the literary, intellectual and cultural sources of racism, sexism and homophobia. But they tended to shy away from anti-Semitism, both because of the mistaken assumption that it was no longer a real problem (after all, Jews were economically and politically flourishing) and because such a confrontation would have forced a challenge to the dominant Western religion at the core of its most dramatic story: the crucifixion.
>
> Nevertheless, since the 1960s there have been thousands of sensitive Christians, who have created a Christian spiritual renewal movement that rejects the teaching of hatred in the Gospel by allegorizing the story and giving greater focus to the resurrection than to the crucifixion. Refocusing attention on the bulk of the Gospel, with its

stories portraying a Jewish Jesus who builds on and elaborates the ancient Torah commandments to "love your neighbor as yourself" and "love the stranger," the Christian renewalists tended to see the 2,000-year history of Christian anti-Semitism as a distortion of the deeper truth of the Gospel.

Ah, yes, "sensitive Christians." In an era in which abortion on demand has been legalized, liberals are simply appalled by the social *faux pas* of insensitivity. Having enthusiastically swallowed a murderous camel, they are bothered by insensitive gnats.

We learn that Jesus was a good Jew, who taught men to love their neighbors as themselves and to love the stranger, as a good Jew should. This one-sided version of both Jesus and Judaism is the product of theological liberalism. As long as movie producers stick to this version of Jesus, liberal Jews will applaud them, and sensitively refrain from mentioning the red ink that these Jesus movies invariably produce.

> So let's understand that the attempt to revive Christian enthusiasm around the part of the story that is focused on cruelty and pain is not only (or even primarily) a threat to the Jews, but rather a threat to all those decent, loving and generous Christians who have found in the Jesus story a foundation for their most humane and caring instincts.

Yes, of course, I almost forgot: "caring instincts." These are the instincts of sensitive people, you understand. Gibson is not sufficiently sensitive and caring. He is not liberal and progressive, either. Neither are Christians who think his movie is successful to the extent that it sticks with the texts of the New Testament. It boils down to this: *Gibson is just not Jewish enough.*

> In a deeper way, the Gibson movie is likely to stimulate a broader assault on all of us who seek to build a world based on caring and love, cooperation and generosity, by giving strength to the part within each of us that despairs, the voice inside each of us that feels that there is no point in struggling to transform the world because it is too hopeless

and too dominated by craziness. Part of the struggle is to reclaim and reaffirm the Jewish Jesus, the Jesus who retains hope for building love right here, the Jesus who unabashedly proclaims that the Kingdom of Heaven has arrived—which is to say that the world right now can be based on love and kindness. It is this voice of Jesus that "The Passion" movie seeks to marginalize or make invisible.[19]

In summary, the Gospels were deliberately slanted by the writers, who wanted to blame the Jews for what the Romans had done; the Chistian churches have not had the courage to admit this; the crucifixion story has produced anti-Semitism; Jesus was Jewish to the extent that He was good, but gentile churches refuse to admit this; liberal theology is caring and sensitive; and Gibson refuses to accept any of this.

No wonder the movie made $300 million in the first month.

"And on Our Children. . . ."

The most offending New Testament passage, we are told by Gibson's critics, is this one: ,

> When Pilate saw that he could prevail nothing, but that rather a tumult was made, he took water, and washed his hands before the multitude, saying, I am innocent of the blood of this just person: see ye to it. Then answered all the people, and said, His blood be on us, and on our children (Matthew 27:24–25).

This passage has been misused by Christians in the past. They have leveled the accusation of "Christ-killers" against contemporary Jews. They have interpreted the phrase, "and on our children," as an open-ended condemnation, what I would call a covenantal condemnation.

Christians have not understood that this inter-generational maledictory oath of the crowd was illegal. The Mosaic law prohibited any such curse.

> The fathers shall not be put to death for the children, neither shall the children be put to death for the fathers: every man shall be put to death for his own sin (Deuteronomy 24:16).

This law could not be more clear. The oath recorded in Matthew's Gospel had no binding power judicially, then or now. The Bible is clear: no father and no group of fathers possess the God-given authority to bind their descendants as unnamed co-conspirators in any unlawful act.

Christians who have not known their Old Testament well, or who have regarded biblical law as irrelevant, have too often believed in the binding authority of this oath, and have then misapplied it. In centuries past, this passage was used to persecute Jews. This was illegitimate then, and it would be illegitimate now. So, it is best that Gibson did not put this oath in the subtitles. There is far too much ignorance today about the Mosaic law. Christians believe that the oath was taken by men who were breaking more than one Mosaic law. They should regard this oath as evidence of lawlessness, not as evidence of the judicial complicity of contemporary Jews.

"Every man shall be put to death for his own sin." This is a frightening law. When it comes to unatoned-for guilt, there is plenty to go around. "For whosoever shall keep the whole law, and yet offend in one point, he is guilty of all" (James 2:10). No group has a monopoly on law-breaking (although groups do specialize in particular areas).[20] No group has immunity from God's sanctions against law-breaking.

Conclusion

In matters Judaic, *The Passion* is generally faithful to the New Testament. Its main deviations involve a *reduction* of the level of guilt implied by the New Testament's account. When attacking Gibson's account of the Sanhedrin's arrest, beating, and conviction of Jesus, Jews and humanist critics should show their readers why their criticisms apply exclusively to Gibson's mishandling of the New Testament's texts. But this has not been their primary line of attack. They have attacked what they claim is Gibson's unauthentic interpretation, when the film is in fact quite close to the New Testament's account, especially the subtitles of Jesus' words.

This strategy of criticism is a self-conscious form of deception. It is designed to shield the film's critics from the charge of being anti-Christian, which many of them are. They are hostile to Gibson's historical account of the day's events because they are equally hostile to the New Testament's historical account. But a frontal assault against the New Testament would reveal the truth: they are not religiously neutral movie critics who are hostile merely to Gibson's uniquely distorted view of Jesus. They are in fact deeply committed anti-Christian zealots who are hostile to the Jesus who is portrayed in the New Testament. They have spent their adult lives being enraged at the New Testament. They are now being disingenuous. They hide their contempt for the New Testament under convenient camouflage: the allegedly misleading subtitles of *The Passion*. The main exception is Dr. Patterson, who forthrightly identifies the New Testament as the source of anti-Semitism. His peers are not equally forthright.

What they are saying, loud and clear, is this: Christians have the legal right to believe whatever they want and read the New Testament at home or in church, but when one of them puts the New Testament's account of Jesus' three trials on-screen—the Sanhedrin's, Herod's, and Pilate's—and shows who His accusers were and what they said, where the whole world can see this for the price of a movie ticket, then things have gone too far. "The movie theater is a sanctuary, an artistically holy place. It is no place for Christian propaganda. We must defend what we believe should be a Constitutional provision: the separation of screen and Christianity."

Never before have America's Establishment cultural commentators displayed their intense anti-Christianity this clearly. Never before have Christians seen this so clearly. Never before have Christians had the evidence of the unlevel playing field presented to them so forcefully. They have seen *The Passion*, and they have read the reviews. The cultural disconnect is clearer to more Christians than it has ever been before. Those who have been setting the cultural agenda do not share the faith of the tens of millions of Christians who attend church weekly.

Then, having fired their rhetorical cannons in full public view, the critics watched in horror as the movie became a blockbuster, beginning on opening day. Their cannons turned out to be pop guns. Will Hays, let alone Joe Breen, never made a blunder this big.

There is a scene in a Disney cartoon that I saw in my youth where Mickey Mouse, playing Jack, in his escape from the giant's castle at the top of the beanstalk, tries to tie the shoelaces of the sleeping giant. This wakes up the giant. Now Mickey and Goofy have to make a run for it. Goofy had warned Mickey not to do this. "It's better to leave well enough alone." That was poor grammar but excellent advice. Abraham Foxman and his peers should have left good enough alone. They woke up the giant, who then yelled into the other room, "Hey, Marge, you want to go to a movie tonight? How about *The Passion*?"

To Abraham Foxman, I can do no better than to quote Joseph's words to his brothers in Egypt regarding their decision, seventeen years earlier, to sell him into slavery.

> But as for you, ye thought evil against me; but God meant it unto good, to bring to pass, as it is this day, to save much people alive (Genesis 50:20).

Notes

1. "ADL Concerned Mel Gibson's 'Passion' Could Fuel Anti-Semitism if Released in Present Form" (Aug. 11, 2003). http://tinyurl.com/jpp7

2. Abraham H. Foxman, "Gibson's Passion." http://tinyurl.com/218ay

3. "ADL Letter to Mel Gibson" (March 24, 2003). http://tinyurl.com/3c16w

4. "ADL Concerned Mel Gibson's 'Passion' Could Fuel Anti-Semitism if Released in Present Form" (Aug. 11, 2003). http://tinyurl.com/jpp7

5. Bekhoroth, 6:1, *The Mishnah*, trans., Herbert Danby (New York: Oxford University Press, [1933] 1987), p. 534.

6. Michael Medved, "*The Passion* and the Prejudice: Why I asked the Anti-Defamation League to give Mel Gibson a break," *Christianity Today* (March 2004). http://tinyurl.com/344zv

7. Michael Medved, "Misguided Critics Fall Into The 'Passion' Pit," *Toward Tradition* (no date). http://tinyurl.com/2sagz

8. George Horowitz, *The Spirit of Jewish law* (New York: Central Book Co., [1953] 1963), p. 100.

9. *Ibid*., p. 101.

10. Medved, "*The Passion* and the Prejudice," op. cit.

11. *Ibid*.

12. See Chapter 8.

13. Daniel Lapin, "Protesting Gibson's Passion Lacks Moral Legitimacy," *Toward Tradition* (Sept. 22, 2003). http://tinyurl.com/2fchc

14. Charles Patterson, "A Whiff of Auschwitz: Mel Gibson and the Gospel of Anti-Semitism," *The Jewish Press* (Feb. 18, 2004). http://tinyurl.com/2efsf

15. Daniel Jonah Goldhagen, "Mel Gibson's Cross of Vengeance," *Forward* (no date). http://tinyurl.com/2m9tc

16. Lee Siegel, "All Politics is Cosmic," *Atlantic Monthly* (June 1996). http://tinyurl.com/2fyon See also the PBS interview of Lerner by David Gergen (June 6, 1996). http://tinyurl.com/27xj5

17. "Hillary Clinton's Politics of Meaning Speech," *Tikkun* (May 1993).

18. Carsten Peter Thiede and Matthew D'Anconia, *Eyewitness to Jesus: Amazing New Manuscript Evidence About the Origin of the Gospels* (New York: Doubleday, 1996).

19. Michael Lerner, "Mel Gibson revives an old message of hate..." *International Herald Tribune* (March 31, 2004). http://tinyurl.com/3262k

20. There are very few African-American pornographers. There are very few Jewish car thieves. There are very few Christian counterfeiters. (Actually, I once employed one. He even used my printing press. He was not very good at his work. He was soon caught, green-handed.)

2

The Outraged New York Times

These things I command you, that ye love one another. If the world hate you, ye know that it hated me before it hated you. If ye were of the world, the world would love his own: but because ye are not of the world, but I have chosen you out of the world, therefore the world hateth you. Remember the word that I said unto you, The servant is not greater than his lord. If they have persecuted me, they will also persecute you; if they have kept my saying, they will keep yours also. But all these things will they do unto you for my name's sake, because they know not him that sent me. If I had not come and spoken unto them, they had not had sin: but now they have no cloke for their sin. He that hateth me hateth my Father also. If I had not done among them the works which none other man did, they had not had sin: but now have they both seen and hated both me and my Father. But this cometh to pass, that the word might be fulfilled that is written in their law, They hated me without a cause (John 15:17–25).

JESUS WARNED THE disciples to expect trouble in the future. After all, He was about to experience more trouble than any man had ever experienced—from the Jews, from the Romans, and from God the Father. He was about to pay God's judicial penalty for the sins of the world—and yours, if you are willing to accept His free gift.[1]

The kind of persecution that Mel Gibson has experienced at the hands of the Establishment media is nothing compared to what the disciples experienced. He knows this. But the basic principle remains true: those who hate the God of the Bible also hate Christ, and those who hate Christ hate His disciples when they openly profess Christ as the only way to salvation. Mel Gibson knew this when he first decided to make *The Passion*, and his suspicions have been confirmed.

In flashbacks, the movie shows Jesus saying these words:

> I am the way, the truth, and the life: no man cometh unto the Father, but by me (John 14:6).

This statement drew the proverbial line in the sand. All those who deny this principle are on one side. All those who affirm it are on the other. This fact alienates—and sometimes outrages—all those who hate the idea of a God who brings final judgment on every person in terms of this declaration. This declaration, if true, divides mankind forever into two groups, the saved and the lost, the sheep and the goats. So, those who want to divide mankind into other rival categories in history, but with no such division in eternity, do what they can to ridicule and even suppress those who affirm Jesus' declaration. They are appalled by the idea of final judgment. These words stick in their craw:

> And I saw a great white throne, and him that sat on it, from whose face the earth and the heaven fled away; and there was found no place for them. And I saw the dead, small and great, stand before God; and the books were opened: and another book was opened, which is the book of life: and the dead were judged out of those things which were written in the books, according to their works. And the sea gave up the dead which were in it; and death and hell delivered up the dead which were in them: and they were judged every man according to

their works. And death and hell were cast into the lake of fire. This is the second death. And whosoever was not found written in the book of life was cast into the lake of fire (Revelation 20:11–15).

This is the underlying motivation of the criticisms of *The Passion* that have appeared in the mainstream news media, especially the editorial opinion pages. There is no doctrine so reviled today by the humanists who dominate the media as the doctrine of final judgment by the God of the Bible. They recognize that *The Passion* had made this division clearer than any previous Hollywood movie. They did what they could before the movie was released to savage it. Now that it has proven to be a blockbuster, they are even more outraged. Tens of millions of people have gone to see this movie. So far, they seem to be satisfied.

What I find fascinating is the fact that full-time movie critics in the larger newspapers gave it better than passing marks. On Yahoo's site, the listed critics gave it a B-. The viewers gave it an A-. But on the Rotten Tomatoes Web site, which includes reviews of less well-known publications and basically unknown reviewers, the ratings were far worse.

Most of the truly savage reviews have been written by people who are not full-time movie critics. The political columnists have crossed over to offer a firestorm of criticism. They understand the culture war and its high stakes better than their colleagues who write movie reviews full-time, and who are more interested in artistry in a film than they are in the struggle to shape culture in general. Thus, we find that the most widely known movie critic, the Pulitzer Prize-winning Roger Ebert of the *Chicago Sun-Times*, gave the movie a four-asterisk rating, his highest, which he rarely does.[2] Ebert is a former screenwriter.

In contrast are the politically correct columnists of the *New York Times*.

The Newspaper of Record

The *New York Times* is often referred to as the newspaper of record in the United States. This assessment is correct. This is because the *Times*' owners two generations ago recognized that any newspaper that expects to be quoted by historians and researchers must provide a comprehensive index. The index for the *New York Times* is more comprehensive than any other American newspaper. It is the only index in most university libraries for any American newspaper. Then the *Times* puts every page of every issue on microfilm. Universities without this microfilm collection are not regarded as serious academic institutions. Thus, historians and academic researchers turn first to the index and the microfilms of the *New York Times* for details of any event. Whatever is published in the *Times* sets the initial frame of reference.

The space devoted by the *Times* to a consideration of *The Passion of the Christ* is simply astounding. If you go to the search engine on the *Times'* Web site, and type in "The Passion" and "Mel Gibson," you will get hundreds of entries. Some of them are repeated more than once—a failure of the search engine—but the list is so large that it will take you an hour to go through them. Most of them are offered for sale. They are not available for free in full-text mode.

The *Times* has an arrangement with the *International Herald Tribune*, which publishes articles and reviews from the *Times*. These articles remain on the Web in full-text mode. Thus, I cite these *IHT* articles whenever I can. You can more easily verify what I say by going to the *IHT*'s site.

A. O. Scott

Scott is a film reviewer. I find it interesting that in his first review (Jan. 30, 2004), he stuck to the issue of movies and movie tradition. He was content to discuss the movie in terms of previous Hollywood movies about Jesus. He ended it with these words:

> But at a certain point, disciples of cinema, whatever their other loyalties, must reaffirm a basic creed: For God's sake, shut up and watch the movie.[3]

But in his February 25 review, published on the day the movie opened, and therefore written before it opened, he took off the kid gloves.

"The Passion of the Christ" is so relentlessly focused on the savagery of Jesus' final hours that this film seems to arise less from love than from wrath, and to succeed more in assaulting the spirit than in uplifting it. Mr. Gibson has constructed an unnerving and painful spectacle that is also, in the end, a depressing one. It is disheartening to see a film made with evident and abundant religious conviction that is at the same time so utterly lacking in grace.

This has become one of the three most common criticisms of the film: its supposed anti-Semitism, its violence, and a lack of focus on the broader teachings of Jesus, which are said to be mostly concerned with love. Yet Scott really does understand the reason for the violence. He understands that the on-screen violence is not gratuitous.

By rubbing our faces in the grisly reality of Jesus' death and fixing our eyes on every welt and gash on his body, this film means to make literal an event that the Gospels often treat with circumspection and that tends to be thought about somewhat abstractly. Look, the movie seems to insist, when we say he died for our sins, this is what we mean.

He then calls this "fathomless cruelty."

But without their fathomless cruelty, the story would not reach its necessary end. To halt the execution would thwart divine providence and refuse the gift of redemption.

Yet he nevertheless goes on to compare the violence of this film with other violent films.

And Mr. Gibson, either guilelessly or ingeniously, has exploited the popular appetite for terror and gore for what he and his allies see as a higher end. The means, however, are no different from those used by virtuosos of shock cinema like Quentin Tarantino and Gaspar Noe, who subjected Ms. Bellucci to such grievous indignity in "Irreversible."

Mr. Gibson is temperamentally a more stolid, less formally adventurous filmmaker, but he is no less a connoisseur of violence, and it will be amusing to see some of the same scolds who condemned Mr. Tarantino's "Kill Bill: Vol. 1" sing the praises of "The Passion of the Christ."

Do you see what he is doing here? He understands that the violence in Gibson's film has to do with the violence associated with redemption. It ultimately has to do with a God who threatens eternal fiery damnation to those who reject Jesus' substitutionary atonement on the cross. Yet he compares the film with the violence of gangster films. He is either trying to confuse his readers or else he has adopted some view of life in which violence as such is in fact a healing power, that is, violence as a redemptive force.

The first part, which takes place in the murk and gloom of night (shot by the superb cinematographer Caleb Deschanel), has the feel of a horror movie. As Jesus prays in the garden of Gethsemane, the camera tiptoes around him like a stalker, and John Debney's score is a high-toned creep show of menacing orchestral undertones and spine-jabbing choral effects. A slithery, effeminate Satan (played, the end credits reveal, by a woman named Rosalinda Celentano) slinks around like something in a Wes Craven nightmare, and Judas, reeling from his betrayal, is menaced by demon children with pointy teeth and milky eyes.

Got that? *The Passion* as a horror flick. But this is only the beginning. He continues:

When daylight dawns, the mood shifts from horror-movie suspense to slasher-film dread.

A horror film slides downward into a slasher film. These two movie styles are the lowest on Hollywood's totem pole of prestige. (The purely pornographic film is not on the totem pole. Pornographic movie production is the specialty of Chatsworth, California, and is mainly on videotape.)

Scott at least refrains from the accusation of gratuitous anti-Semitism.

Is "The Passion of the Christ" anti-Semitic? I thought you'd never ask. To my eyes it did not seem to traffic explicitly or egregiously in the toxic iconography of historical Jew hatred, but more sensitive viewers may disagree. The Pharisees, in their tallit and beards, are certainly shown as a sinister and inhumane group, and the mob they command is full of howling, ugly rage. But this on-screen villainy does not seem to exceed what can be found in the source material.

The key sentence is this one: "But this on-screen villainy does not seem to exceed what can be found in the source material." This is what the horde of critics who have accused the movie of anti-Semitism rarely mention. They instead single out Gibson's interpretation as the source of the problem.

What makes the movie so grim and ugly is Mr. Gibson's inability to think beyond the conventional logic of movie narrative. In most movies—certainly in most movies directed by or starring Mr. Gibson—violence against the innocent demands righteous vengeance in the third act, an expectation that Mr. Gibson in this case whips up and leaves unsatisfied.

Let me point to the obvious: the movie is about the death of Jesus, not the post-resurrection events. Nevertheless, the movie does emphasize the words of Jesus on the cross.

Father, forgive them, for they know not what they do (Luke 23:34).

The movie goes beyond the New Testament's texts by having the forgiven thief on the cross call out to the High Priest that this grant of mercy applies to him. And it did. It applied to the Romans, too. This is the whole point of Jesus' declaration. The victim in Mosaic law had the legal right to offer forgiveness to the criminal.[4] Oblivious to any of this, Scott ends his review with these words.

On its own, apart from whatever beliefs a viewer might bring to it, "The Passion of the Christ" never provides a clear sense of what all of this bloodshed was for, an inconclusiveness that is Mr. Gibson's most serious artistic failure. The Gospels, at least in some interpretations, suggest that the story ends in forgiveness. But such an ending seems beyond Mr. Gibson's imaginative capacities. Perhaps he suspects that his public prefers terror, fury and gore.[5]

This is simply astounding. Gibson's public, meaning the Christian component of his audience, knows that without the sacrificial atonement by Jesus, all that any of us has a legitimate right to look forward to in eternity is terror, fury, and gore. That portion of his public that does not believe this, Gibson is trying to persuade. Like every passion play, this one is a tool of Christian evangelism. The movie's critics know this, and they hate this movie with a special hatred, for it brings this evangelical message to the screen, where a hundred million people may see it before it goes to DVD, after which a billion people may see it.

Frank Rich

He has written repeatedly about *The Passion*. In his August 1, 2003 column, he referred to groups of Jews and Catholics who had seen a preliminary script and had warned against it. The language of this warning, let it be noted, is almost identical to Abraham Foxman's three-fold assessment, which I referred to in the previous chapter.

Eventually, Gibson's film will have to face audiences he doesn't cherry-pick. We can only hope that the finished product will not resemble the screenplay that circulated this spring. That script—which the Gibson camp has said was stolen but which others say was leaked by a concerned member of the star's own company—received thumbs down from a panel of nine Jewish and Roman Catholic scholars who read it. They found that Jews were presented as "bloodthirsty, vengeful and money-hungry," reported The Jewish Week, which broke the story of the scholars' report in June.

He then goes on to argue that Gibson started warning against Jewish opposition before the movie had begun production. Rich sees this as a public relations ploy. Yet he also admits that Jews have indeed opposed the film. He ended his article contemptuously.

> But the real question here is why Gibson and his minions would go out of their way to bait Jews and sow religious conflict, especially at this fragile historical moment. It's enough to make you pray for the second coming of Charlton Heston.[6]

In a follow-up, article, "'Passion' and the U.S. culture war" (March 5, 2004), he refers to—you will love this—the movie's "orgasmic spurting of blood." This is just another reviewer doing his best to offer a faithful artistic judgment of a new film.

> With its laborious build-up to its orgasmic spurtings of blood and other bodily fluids, the film is constructed like nothing so much as a porn movie, replete with slo-mo climaxes and pounding music. Of all the "Passion" critics, no one has nailed its artistic vision more precisely than the journalist Christopher Hitchens, who called it a homoerotic "exercise in lurid sadomasochism" for those who "like seeing handsome young men stripped and flayed alive over a long period of time."

I will deal with Hitchens' review in the next chapter. That Rich agrees with it tells us a great deal about Rich. In his next assessment, he refers to Leni Riefenstahl, who had died a few months earlier at the age of 101. She had directed the Nazi propaganda film, *The Triumph of the Will*, in 1933. Linking her name with Gibson's is not what I would call an above-the-belt blow.

> As a director, Gibson is no Leni Riefenstahl. His movie is just too ponderous to spark a pogrom on its own—in America anyway. The one ugly incident reported on Ash Wednesday, in which the Lovingway United Pentecostal Church posted a marquee reading "Jews Killed the Lord Jesus," occurred in Denver, where the local archbishop, Charles

Chaput, had thrown kindling on the fire by promoting the movie for months. Whether "The Passion" will prove quite as benign in Europe and the Arab world is a story yet to be told.

Again, this reference to Europe and the Arab world is typical. As Rabbi Lapin has pointed out, the Jews' problem is not with Christians; it is with Muslims. The critics' conclusion is that Christians must not make movies about the crucifixion of Jesus because Muslims may attack Jews after seeing the movie. Here we have the great reversal of the liberals' age-old refrain: "Movies do not cause post-screening evil actions by viewers; they merely entertain."

My question is this: Why will fanatical Muslims welcome a movie about the death and resurrection of Jesus? Why will they be pleased with a movie that faithfully presents Jesus' words before the High Priest that affirmed His position as the son of God? I hope they will believe this movie's message, but I am not optimistic.

Rich escalates his rhetoric.

But speaking as someone who has never experienced serious bigotry, I must confess that, whatever happens abroad, the fracas over "The Passion" has made me feel less secure as a Jew in America than ever before. My quarrel is not with most of the millions of Christian believers who are moved to tears by "The Passion." They bring their own deep feelings to the theater with them, and when Gibson pushes their buttons, however crudely, they generously do his work for him, supplying from their hearts the authentic spirituality that is missing in his jamboree of bloody beefcake.

I assume that you have seen the movie. Would you assess it as a "jamboree of bloody beefcake"? The actor who played Jesus did not impress me as "beefcake."

What concerns me much more are those with leadership positions in the secular world—including those in the media—who have given

Gibson, "The Passion" and its most incendiary hucksters a free pass for behavior that is unambiguously contrived to vilify Jews.

Start with the movie itself. There is no question that it rewrites history by making Caiaphas and the other high priests the prime instigators of Jesus' death while softening Pontius Pilate, an infamous Roman thug, into a reluctant and somewhat conscience-stricken executioner.

I ask in response: "What do the New Testament texts say about Pilate?"

Pilate saith unto them, What shall I do then with Jesus which is called Christ? They all say unto him, Let him be crucified. And the governor said, Why, what evil hath he done? But they cried out the more, saying, Let him be crucified. When Pilate saw that he could prevail nothing, but that rather a tumult was made, he took water, and washed his hands before the multitude, saying, I am innocent of the blood of this just person: see ye to it. Then answered all the people, and said, His blood be on us, and on our children. Then released he Barabbas unto them: and when he had scourged Jesus, he delivered him to be crucified (Matthew 27:22–26).

Then said Pilate to the chief priests and to the people, I find no fault in this man. And they were the more fierce, saying, He stirreth up the people, teaching throughout all Jewry, beginning from Galilee to this place (Luke 23:4–5).

Rich here adopts a tactic repeated again and again by the critics. *He blames Gibson for the New Testament's version of the event.* Rabbi Lapin understands this tactic, and he warns about its consequences.

Do we really want to open up the Pandora's Box of suggesting that any faith may demand the removal of material that it finds offensive from the doctrines of any other faith? Do we really want to return to those dark times when Catholic authorities attempted to strip from the Talmud those passages that they found offensive? Some of my Jewish readers may feel squeamish about my alluding to the existence of

Talmudic passages uncomplimentary toward Jesus as well as descriptive of Jewish involvement in his crucifixion. However the truth is that anyone with Internet access can easily locate those passages in about ten seconds. I think it far better that in the name of genuine Jewish-Christian friendship in America, we allow all faiths their own beliefs even if we find those beliefs troubling or at odds with our own beliefs. This way we can all prosper safely under the constitutional protection of the United States of America.[7]

For the sake of the peace, he argues, Jews should cease their tactic of trying to call into question Gibson's movie. But he aims his recommendation to practicing Jews. Non-practicing Jews had not paid attention. Rich paid no attention.

As if that weren't enough, the Jewish high priests are also depicted as grim sadists with bad noses and teeth—Shylocks and Fagins from 19th-century stock. Yet in those early screenings that Gibson famously threw for conservative politicos in Washington last summer and autumn, not a person in attendance, from Robert Novak to Peggy Noonan, seems to have recognized these obvious stereotypes, let alone spoken up about them in their profuse encomiums to the film.

Bad teeth? Bad noses? I saw the movie twice. Like Novak and Noonan, I did not notice this, either.

He then comes to the heart of the matter with respect to the impact of the movie: the culture war.

The vilification of Jews by Gibson, his film and some of his allies, unchallenged by his media enablers, is not happening in a vacuum. We are in the midst of an escalating election-year culture war in which those of "faith" are demonizing so-called secularists—any Jews critical of Gibson and their fellow travelers, liberals.

Gibson has "media enablers." How terrible! Apparently, they failed. The wave of outrage by media pundits has been nearly universal, especially in the *New York Times*. Rich sees the war primarily in political terms. This reveals the operational worldview of our opponents. They see everything as political. They believe in political salvation, so they also believe in political damnation.

> But when even Connecticut's John Rowland, a scandal-ridden governor facing impeachment, starts to rave about "The Passion" in public ("unbelievable!" "breathtaking!"), as he did last weekend, it's clear that we're witnessing the birth of a phenomenon. You come away from this whole sorry story feeling that Jesus died in "The Passion of the Christ" so cynics, whether seeking bucks or votes, could inherit the earth.[8]

He is correct about one thing: we are witnessing the birth of a phenomenon. The victims are waking up. They have been asleep longer than Rip Van Winkle.

Cheaper by the Dozen

On the *Times'* site, we find a short list of reviews and comments on the movie. Most of these articles are archived, so they may be purchased. You get a discount if you buy a dozen of them. Far be it from me to suppress information that may add revenue to The Newspaper of Record. The *Times* devoted the following links to articles: "Spotlight on 'The Passion of the Christ.'"[9] So here, without editorial comment, I reproduce the list.[10] You can see for yourself the general thrust of their message. See what Gibson was up against.

MOVIE REVIEW / 'THE PASSION OF THE CHRIST'
Good and Evil Locked in Violent Showdown
By A. O. SCOTT
Mel Gibson's film is so relentlessly focused on the savagery of Jesus' final hours that it succeeds more in assaulting the spirit than in uplifting it. (Feb. 25, 2004)

ARTS & IDEAS

What Did Jesus Really Look Like?

By DAVID GIBSON

From Eastern Orthodox icons to Hollywood movie hunks, depictions of Jesus have always served the needs of the day. (Feb. 21, 2004)

ARTS & LEISURE

'The Passion's' Precedent: The Most-Watched Film Ever?

By FRANKLIN FOER

"Jesus," a 1979 Warner Brothers release, is all but forgotten in Hollywood, but it is sometimes described as the most watched movie of all time. (Feb. 8, 2004)

CRITIC'S NOTEBOOK

Enraged Filmgoers: The Wages of Faith?

By A. O. SCOTT

The advent of Mel Gibson's "Passion of the Christ" has brought with it a controversy that seems, at least at first glance, familiar, even ritualistic. (Jan. 30, 2004)

WEEK IN REVIEW

Seeing and Believing: A Movie's Power Over Attitudes and Action

By JANET MASLIN

Movies spawn fads and fashions, but can they change attitudes? Mel Gibson's graphic re-enactment of the Crucifixion may offer some answers. (Feb. 22, 2004)

EDITORIALS/OP-ED

Not Peace, but a Sword

By WILLIAM SAFIRE

Mel Gibson's reactionary version of the suffering of Jesus, which provokes outrage and casts blame, fails Christian and Jew. (March 1, 2004)

Peter, Paul, Mary . . . and God

By NICHOLAS D. KRISTOF

A lost proto-feminist text, "Gospel of Mary of Magdala," offers a more provocative look at early Christianity than even "The Passion." (Feb. 28, 2004)

Stations of the Crass?

By MAUREEN DOWD

You should come out of the theater suffused with charity toward your fellow man. But this is a Mel Gibson film, so you come out wanting to kick someone's teeth in. (Feb. 26, 2004)

Do You Recognize This Jesus?

By KENNETH L. WOODWARD

The evangelical Christians who will flock to "The Passion of the Christ" are in for a shocking refresher in the forgotten basics of Christianity. (Feb. 25, 2004)

EACTIONS

For One Catholic, 'Passion' Skews the Meaning of the Crucifixion

By MARY GORDON

My problem with "The Passion of the Christ" is that I felt as if I were being continually hit over the head with a two-by-four. (Feb. 28, 2004)

Agreed: All the Publicity Is a Triumph for 'Passion'

By RANDY KENNEDY

The experts who gathered for a public discussion of Mel Gibson's film agreed he had succeeded, at least, in creating a frenzy. (Feb. 28, 2004)

Long-Awaited Film Draws Passionate Crowds Around the U.S.

By LAURIE GOODSTEIN

As if on pilgrimage, moviegoers around the country flocked to theaters on Ash Wednesday to see the opening of "The Passion of the Christ." (Feb. 26, 2004)

'Passion' Disturbs a Panel of Religious Leaders

By LAURIE GOODSTEIN

An interfaith panel of eight Christian and Jewish clergy members and laypeople who gathered to watch "The Passion of the Christ" emerged disturbed by the film. (Feb. 25, 2004)

Tears and Gasps for 'Passion' (and Oh, All That Blood)

By JAMES BARRON

Mel Gibson's "Passion of the Christ" was shown on Feb. 23 at screenings in New York and New Jersey. (Feb. 23, 2004)

Some Christians See 'Passion' as Evangelism Tool

By LAURI GOODSTEIN

Christians nationwide are busy preparing to use "The Passion of the Christ" in an immense evangelistic campaign. (Feb. 5, 2004)

Gibson to Delete a Scene in 'The Passion'

By SHARON WAXMAN

Mel Gibson, responding to focus groups and Jewish critics, will delete a controversial scene about Jews from "The Passion of the Christ." (Feb. 4, 2004)

Jewish Leaders Upset After Viewing 'Passion'

By RANDY KENNEDY

Two of the nation's most prominent Jewish leaders found recent versions of "The Passion of the Christ" to be anti-Semitic and incendiary. (Jan. 23, 2004)

Months Before Debut, Movie on Death of Jesus Causes Stir

By LAURIE GOODSTEIN

With his movie under attack as anti-Semitic, Mel Gibson is trying to build a defense before it is released. (Aug. 2, 2003)

FRANK RICH COLUMNS

The Pope's Thumbs Up for Gibson's 'Passion'

By FRANK RICH

The marketing of "The Passion of the Christ" plugs into the spiritual McCarthyism of our cultural moment. It demeans the Pope to be drafted into the scheme. (Jan. 18, 2004)

The Greatest Story Ever Sold
By FRANK RICH

The contentious rollout of Mel Gibson's movie has resembled a political, rather than a spiritual, campaign. (Sept. 21, 2003)

Mel Gibson's Martyrdom Complex
By FRANK RICH

Mel Gibson's new privately financed movie is sowing religious conflict. (Aug. 3, 2003)

ABOUT MEL GIBSON
New Film May Harm Gibson's Career
By SHARON WAXMAN

Mel Gibson's provocative new film, "The Passion of the Christ," is making some of Hollywood's most prominent executives uncomfortable in ways that may damage Mr. Gibson's career. (Feb. 26, 2004)

Word for Word: The Passion of Mel Gibson
By KARI HASKELL

Mel Gibson weighs in on several points about his new movie, "The Passion of the Christ," and his father, who has belittled the Holocaust and railed against Jews. (Feb. 22, 2004)

Mel Gibson's Longstanding Movie Martyr Complex
By ELVIS MITCHELL

Eyes often misted over with anguish and sorrow, Mel Gibson has been martyred on screen more often and more photogenically than anyone since Joan Crawford. (Feb. 8, 2004)

Is the Pope Catholic Enough?
By CHRISTOPHER NOXON

Mel Gibson is making a movie about Jesus and he's financing an ul-traconservative church near Los Angeles. His father couldn't be proud-er—but his views may be even more unorthodox. (March 9, 2003)

Conclusion

I could go on, citing more extracts, making more comments, but do I need to? There is an old line, "You don't have to eat all of a rotten apple to know it's rotten." The Newspaper of Record has made itself clear. It does not like *The Passion of the Christ*.

What the *Times* published, its imitators have published. Abraham Foxman set the agenda. The *Times* promoted the agenda. The rest of the Establishment media followed suit.

Notes

1. Gary North, *Unconditional Surrender: God's Program for Victory*, 3rd ed. (Tyler, Texas: Institute for Christian Economics, 1988), ch. 2. Available free on www.freebooks.com.

2. Roger Ebert, "The Passion of the Christ," *Chicago-Sun Times* (Feb. 24, 2004). http://tinyurl.com/34gkh

3. A. O. Scott, "Christ and controversy, a Hollywood rite," *International Herald Tribune* (Jan. 30, 2004). http://tinyurl.com/2f36g

4. Gary North, *Victim's Rights: The Biblical View of Civil Justice* (Tyler, Texas: Institute for Christian Economics, 1990). Available free on www.freebooks.com.

5. A. O. Scott, "More wrath than love infuses Mel Gibson's [Passion]" *International Herald Tribune* (no date) http://tinyurl.com/2zg33

6. Frank Rich, "The gospel according to Gibson," *International Herald Tribune* (Aug. 1, 2003). http://tinyurl.com/2mrxn

7. Daniel Lapin, "Protesting Gibson's Passion Lacks Moral Legitimacy," *Toward Tradition* (Sept. 22, 2003). http://tinyurl.com/2fchc

8. Frank Rich, "'Passion' and the U.S. Culture war," *International Herald Tribune* (March 5, 2004) http://tinyurl.com/yvmjy

9. http://tinyurl.com/25pgq

10. "Spotlight on 'The Passion of the Christ,'" *New York Times*. http://tinyurl.com/25pqg

3

Following the Leader

For we have not followed cunningly devised fables, when we made known unto you the power and coming of our Lord Jesus Christ, but were eyewitnesses of his majesty (II Peter 1:16).

PETER ADDRESSED WHAT had already become a problem for the church. Critics had accused them of following fables. The crowd at Athens responded to Paul's presentation of the gospel of redemption through faith in Christ:

> And the times of this ignorance God winked at; but now commandeth all men every where to repent: Because he hath appointed a day, in the which he will judge the world in righteousness by that man whom he hath ordained; whereof he hath given assurance unto all men, in that he hath raised him from the dead. And when they heard of the resurrection of the dead, some mocked: and others said, We will hear thee again of this matter. So Paul departed from among them (Acts 17:30–33).

There are always mockers. We live in an era in which the mockers control the major media. But they are beginning to lose control over the levers of public opinion. The Internet has undermined their near-monopoly. So has talk radio. The networks are losing market share every year. The profits are disappearing. About the only place remaining where there is still a near-monopoly for the scoffers is the movie industry.

Now comes Mel Gibson, who threatens to tell the old, old story to a billion people. The mockers became worried as soon as they heard about the project. They did their best to stop its production. Then they tried to get him to change it. Then they said it would flop. They have been beaten, step by step, along their own *via dolorosa*.

The Catholic League for Religious and Civil Rights has put on-line extracts from dozens of the movie's critics, along with rebuttals from Catholic and other sources.[1] Here, I concentrate on some of the more widely cited critics.

David Denby

Whatever the *New York Times* establishes as conventional becomes acceptable to the rest of the journals of Establishment opinion. Whatever license the *Times* takes with the truth, the also-rans and wanna-be's are ready to affirm.

The New Yorker is surely a wanna-be, or more accurately, a wanna-be-again. There was a time, sixty years ago, when *The New Yorker* was a trend-setter. Under the editorship of the amazing Harold Ross, a small army of authors established literary careers.[2] But the magazine has fallen on hard times. The extent of this erosion can be seen clearly in the review of *The Passion* by David Denby. Ross would not have let it get into print. It appears in the March 1 issue.

Denby begins with what has become a standard tactic. He praises the Jesus of theological liberalism. This Jesus is not the Jesus of the Apostles' Creed, let alone the Nicene Creed. He is not very God of very God, born of a virgin, who will come again in final judgment to judge both the quick and the dead. Jesus is instead the teacher who never claimed to be God, who stands as an ethical beacon, and whose words to the contrary were added by later "redactors," which is a fancy academic word for "forgers."

In "The Passion of the Christ," Mel Gibson shows little interest in celebrating the electric charge of hope and redemption that Jesus Christ brought into the world. He largely ignores Jesus' heart-stopping eloquence, his startling ethical radicalism and personal radiance—Christ as a "paragon of vitality and poetic assertion," as John Updike described Jesus' character in his essay "The Gospel According to Saint Matthew."

When it comes to understanding Jesus, Mr. Denby thinks we should turn to John Updike in preference to Matthew, the latter of whom recorded Jesus' words:

And fear not them which kill the body, but are not able to kill the soul: but rather fear him which is able to destroy both soul and body in hell (Matthew 10:28).

Whosoever therefore shall confess me before men, him will I confess also before my Father which is in heaven. But whosoever shall deny me before men, him will I also deny before my Father which is in heaven. Think not that I am come to send peace on earth: I came not to send peace, but a sword. For I am come to set a man at variance against his father, and the daughter against her mother, and the daughter in law against her mother in law. And a man's foes shall be they of his own household. He that loveth father or mother more than me is not worthy of me: and he that loveth son or daughter more than me is not worthy of me. And he that taketh not his cross, and followeth after me, is not worthy of me (Matthew 10:32–38).

Mel Gibson, in Mr. Denby's opinion, has done a despicable thing. He has portrayed Jesus' message as one of hate. Yes, it may be true that the New Testament's texts record that the Sanhedrin beat Jesus. The Roman soldiers first beat Him, then they crucified Him, at the specific demand of the Jews. But Mr. Denby regards Gibson as the culprit here. His essay is titled, "Nailed."

As a viewer, I am equally free to say that the movie Gibson has made from his personal obsessions is a sickening death trip, a grimly unilluminating procession of treachery, beatings, blood, and agony—and to say so without indulging in "anti-Christian sentiment" (Gibson's term for what his critics are spreading). For two hours, with only an occasional pause or gentle flashback, we watch, stupefied, as a handsome, strapping, at times half-naked young man (James Caviezel) is slowly tortured to death. Gibson is so thoroughly fixated on the scourging and crushing of Christ, and so meagrely involved in the spiritual meanings of the final hours, that he falls in danger of altering Jesus' message of love into one of hate.

And against whom will the audience direct its hate? As Gibson was completing the film, some historians, theologians, and clergymen accused him of emphasizing the discredited charge that it was the ancient Jews who were primarily responsible for killing Jesus, a claim that has served as the traditional justification for the persecution of the Jews in Europe for nearly two millennia. The critics turn out to have been right.

As a matter of fact, a little group of liberal Roman Catholic critics and Jews, whose group had no official standing in the Church, did in fact say something like this. They released their statement on June 17, 2003.[3] Because an advanced copy had been supplied to the NCSJ, a Jewish organization, the NCSJ published a summary of the report in the June 13 issue of *The Jewish Week*.

> "A film based on the present version of the script of 'The Passion' would promote anti-Semitic sentiments," according to the "Report of the Ad Hoc Scholars Group," a copy of which was obtained by The Jewish Week.
>
> The group is comprised of nine prominent Catholic and Jewish scholars at major universities across the country who reviewed a copy of the script.[4]

The summary said that there were four Jews on the committee, but the committee's press release, *Dramatizing the Death of Jesus*, mentions only four people, all Catholics. A link to the committee's statement was posted by the Anti-Defamation League on June 24. The press release was still on the ADL's Web site in March, 2004.[5] The members of the group were heralded as experts by secular reviewers. But the humanists in the media failed to report that the Bishops' organization almost immediately had distanced itself from the scholars' committee: on June 11. It said, "Neither the Bishops' Committee for Ecumenical and Interreligious Affairs, nor any other committee of the United States Conference of Catholic Bishops, established this group, or authorized, reviewed or approved the report written by its members."[6] The ad hoc committee had admitted this in its June 17 press release, but the critics failed to mention this fact.

The movie opened February 25. It took in $23.5 million. The next day, the U.S. Conference of Catholic Bishops issued a press release. Here is what the conservative press reported. The Establishment media remained silent.

> The U.S. Conference of Catholic Bishops (USCCB) retracted critical remarks made about the film last April by its ecumenical and interreligious committee, which suggested that the film might be anti-Semitic.
>
> In remarks released Wednesday on Catholic News Service, three staff members of the USCCB's Office for Film and Broadcasting said the film might be overly violent but not anti-Semitic.
>
> "Concerning the issue of anti-Semitism, the Jewish people are at no time blamed collectively for Jesus' death," said a review by Gerri Pare, David DiCerto and Anne Navarro. "Rather, Christ freely embraces his destiny."
>
> The reviewers went on to call the movie "an artistic achievement in terms of its textured cinematography, haunting atmospherics, lyrical editing, detailed production and soulful score."[7]

With this in mind, let us return to Mr. Denby's review.

> At first, the movie looks like a graveyard horror flick, and then, as Jewish temple guards show up bearing torches, like a faintly tedious art film.

This language is reminiscent of Frank Rich's February 25 review: "The first part, which takes place in the murk and gloom of night (shot by the superb cinematographer Caleb Deschanel), has the feel of a horror movie."

Denby is upset because the movie does not conform to the latest findings of liberal theologians, who are referred to by Denby as "others."

> History is also treated selectively. The writer Jon Meacham, in a patient and thorough article in Newsweek, has detailed the many small ways that Gibson disregarded what historians know of the period, with the effect of assigning greater responsibility to the Jews, and less to the Romans, for Jesus' death. Meacham's central thesis, which is shared by others, is that the priests may have been willing to sacrifice Jesus—whose mass following may have posed a threat to Roman governance—in order to deter Pilate from crushing the Jewish community altogether.

The character created by comedian Flip Wilson, Geraldine, was famous for her phrase, "The devil made me do it." Every time she was caught in some transgression, she repeated her line. We see this strategy here. "Pontius Pilate made us do it."

Denby is more forthright than most other reviewers about Gibson's reliance on the New Testament. He says that the text's writers faked the account for political reasons.

> Gibson ignores most of the dismaying political context, as well as the likelihood that the Gospel writers, still under Roman rule, had very practical reasons to downplay the Romans' role in the Crucifixion.

The problem with Gibson, Denby says, is that he is not faithful to the artistic vision of the Renaissance. Denby has great respect for the Renaissance.

> But the central tradition of Italian Renaissance painting left Christ relatively unscathed; the artists emphasized not the physical suffering of the man but the sacrificial nature of his death and the astonishing mystery of his transformation into godhood—the Resurrection and the triumph over carnality. Gibson instructed Deschanel to make the movie look like the paintings of Caravaggio, but in Caravaggio's own "Flagellation of Christ" the body of Jesus is only slightly marked. Even Goya, who hardly shrank from dismemberment and pain in his work, created a "Crucifixion" with a nearly unblemished Jesus. Crucifixion, as the Romans used it, was meant to make a spectacle out of degradation and suffering—to humiliate the victim through the apparatus of torture. By embracing the Roman pageant so openly, using all the emotional resources of cinema, Gibson has cancelled out the redemptive and transfiguring power of art.

The critics are humanists. They do not believe that sinners are in the hands of an angry God. They do not believe that God sacrificed His own Son this way in order to provide a substitute for all those who are willing to affirm their need for a substitute. Jesus' death is the only acceptable substitute. So, the humanists seek redemption in other ways. It is clear what Denby's substitute means of salvation is: art. "Gibson has cancelled out the redemptive and transfiguring power of art." Paint your way to heaven. Sculpt your way out of hell. Besides, there is no hell.

Denby then compares *The Passion* with *The Last Temptation of Christ*. You should be aware of Denby's artistic preference, a preference based on his view of redemption.

> The depictions in "The Passion," one of the cruellest movies in the history of the cinema, are akin to the bloody Pop representation of Jesus found in, say, a roadside shrine in Mexico, where the addition of

an Aztec sacrificial flourish makes the passion a little more passionate. Such are the traps of literal-mindedness. The great modernist artists, aware of the danger of kitsch and the fascination of sado-masochism, have largely withdrawn into austerity and awed abstraction or into fervent humanism, as in Scorsese's "The Last Temptation of Christ" (1988), which features an existential Jesus sorely tried by the difficulty of the task before him. There are many ways of putting Jesus at risk and making us feel his suffering.

That last sentence calls to mind President Clinton's famous remark, "I feel your pain." The author is correct. There are indeed many ways to feel Jesus' suffering. The most effective way is to be consigned to hell. I suggest an alternative. So does Mel Gibson.

Christopher Hitchens

Hitchens is a non-practicing Jew. He did not learn of his Jewish origins until he was 38, when his nonagenarian grandmother informed him. He was happy to hear it. He used to be far-Left politically, but ever since the terrorist attack in 2001, he has moved to an anti-socialist position.[8] He is a professor of Liberal Studies at the New School of Social Research in New York City. It would not come as a surprise to John Bunyan that Hitchens is a columnist for *Vanity Fair*. He is the brother of Britain's conservative columnist, Peter Hitchens, who is also an ex-Marxist.

Hitchens published two reviews of *The Passion*. Both were published on February 27, two days after the movie opened. He must have written them on February 26. The first is aptly titled, "I Detest This Film . . With a Passion." He begins with an outrageous statement that he obviously does not believe, and which attendance figures prove is preposterous.

> Now he has made a film that principally appeals to the gay Christian sado-masochistic community: a niche market that hasn't been sufficiently exploited.

If you like seeing handsome young men stripped and tied up and flayed with whips, The Passion Of The Christ is the movie for you. . . .

In order to keep up this relentless propaganda pressure, Gibson employs the cheap technique of the horror movie director.

Here it is again: The horror movie theme. Yes, this movie is horrifying, but for an aesthetic reason. The execution of Jesus and the beatings that preceded it were horrible.

Hitchens is upset because of the inclusion of the Jews' self-maledictory oath on themselves and their children, which the New Testament recounts.

In a widely publicized concession, Gibson said that he'd removed the scene where the Jewish mob cries out that it wants the blood of Jesus to descend on the heads of its children's children.

This very questionable episode—it is mentioned in only one of the four gospels—has in fact not been cut. Only the English subtitle has gone.

He apparently thinks it is a very big deal that the curse is recorded in "only one" of the gospels, as if this proves that it never took place. He thinks his readers will be impressed. But no reader who believes the New Testament's account of that day will be impressed. One Gospel's account is sufficient.

So when the film is later shown, in Russia and Poland, say, or Egypt and Syria, there will be a ready-made propaganda vehicle for those who fancy a bit of torture and murder, with a heavy dose of Jew-baiting thrown in.

Gibson knows very well that this will happen, and he'll be raking it in from exactly those foreign rights to the film.[9]

Hitchens has to regard the Gospel of Matthew, where the curse is recorded, as Jew-baiting. He has targeted Gibson because he has targeted the Gospel of Matthew. Gibson is a surrogate target—a substitute, in other words.

On the *Slate* site, he closes his second review with this note:

> Now, as the dollars begin to flow from this front-loaded fruit-ma-chine of cynical publicity, he is sobbing about the risks and sacrifices he has made for the Lord. A coward, a bully, a bigmouth, and a queer-basher. Yes, we have been here before. The word is fascism, in case you are wondering, and we don't have to sit through that movie again.[10]

There it is, the ever-present epithet that issues from the mouths and pens and word processors of leftists: *fascism*. Is there one of them who has ever sat down and read an article by Mussolini or Giovinni Gentile (pronounced, of course, genTEElay). I have. Let me assure you that any connection between *The Passion* and fascism is only geographical: the Italian origin of both the Romans and the fascists. Hitchens has not yet thrown off the tactics and the vocabulary of the Left, no matter what he has said to interviewers. For the Left, every opponent is a fascist.

Andy Rooney/Dennis Duggan

Here is a two-for-one review. On the weekend before *The Passion* opened, Andy Rooney did a hatchet job on Gibson. Rooney has a huge audience. He offers the humor segment that closes the CBS-TV documentary news show, *60 Minutes*. He began by targeting Pat Robertson's statement that God had told him that President Bush would be re-elected in a blowout. Robertson, a charismatic, really said this. He was an easy target. Then Rooney began the satire part of his segment.

> I heard from God just the other night. God always seems to call at night.
>
> "Andrew," God said to me. He always calls me "Andrew." I like that.
>
> "Andrew, you have the eyes and ears of a lot of people. I wish you'd tell your viewers that both Pat Robertson and Mel Gibson strike me as wackos. I believe that's one of your current words. They're crazy as

bedbugs, another earthly expression. I created bedbugs. I'll tell you, they're no crazier than people," said God.

"Let me just say that I think I'd remember if I'd ever talked to Pat Robertson, and I'd remember if I said Bush would get re-elected in a blowout."

"As far as Mel Gibson goes, I haven't seen his movie, 'The Passion of the Christ,' because it hasn't opened up here yet. But I did catch Gibson being interviewed by Diane Sawyer. I did something right when I came up with her, didn't I," added God. "Anyway, as I was saying, Mel is a real nut case. What in the world was I thinking when I created him? Listen, we all make mistakes."

Rooney ended the segment with this barb:

My question to Mel Gibson is: "How many million dollars does it look as if you're going to make off the crucifixion of Christ?"[11]

Rooney is a certifiable curmudgeon, more than any other popular TV personality. He is in his 80s. He is an agnostic. He is not interested in supernatural religion. He is a TV version of the proverbial nineteenth-century village atheist.

Two weeks later, *60 Minutes'* co-host Leslie Stahl introduced Rooney's segment of the show by saying that viewers had sent him 30,000 pieces of mail, a record. Most of the letters had to do with Mel Gibson, not Pat Robertson, she said. Then Rooney spent his segment reading some of these letters and adding comments. A few letters were really angry, but most were amusing. Rooney is no fool. He was able to fill his time slot for the week without writing a humor monologue. The letters did it for him.

He began with these words: "I think the mail was a good indication of how bitterly divided our country is right now." This indicates that he is a card-carrying member of the Establishment media. The country is not bitterly divided over *The Passion*. The vast majority of the country remains officially Christian, in sharp contrast to the atheists and humanists who control the media. From time to time, viewers get fed up. This was one of those times. His sample of letters included these.

1. "I am so angry I could spit!!!"

2. "You asinine, bottom-dwelling, numb-skulled, low-life, slimy, sickening, gutless, spineless, ignorant, pot-licking, cowardly pathetic little weasel."

3. "Andy Rooney is a nut case, and should be fined and removed for his obnoxious, sarcastic and vicious comments. . . . Or better yet—he should have his eyebrows shaved off." [Rooney's eyebrows are legendary.]

4. "Andy, please get some help before they find you walking aimlessly on the streets of New York, not knowing where you live or who you are."

5. "I'm not crazy about Mel, and I probably won't go see his movie . . . I want you to know though, Mr. Rooney, I don't like you either."[12]

Rooney was good-natured about it all, just as any self-respecting village atheist should be. But it is clear that neither he nor the producer of *60 Minutes* had suspected two weeks earlier just how outraged viewers would be. Television people, like their spiritual compatriots in Hollywood, live in a hermetically sealed-off world where hardly anyone goes to church regularly and almost everyone in New York City's sphere of influence reads the Sunday *New York Times* instead.

Dennis Duggan of *Newsday* picked up Rooney's lead on the day before *The Passion* opened. His title: "God to Mel: You're a nut."

It must be going around.

What I mean is God has been talking to me lately. Just as he has been talking to Mel Gibson, the Rev. Pat Robertson and Andy Rooney, who said on "60 Minutes" Sunday that God told him Gibson is "wacko" and "crazy as a bedbug."

This is what God told me.

"See this movie about my Son real quick. I don't think it's going to be playing past next week," God said.

Here, the writer displays his monumental misunderstanding of Americans and their commitment to God. The movie opened the next day with blockbuster status.

"A sickening death trip," wrote David Denby of the New Yorker, which pretty much captures the overall flavor of the reviews.

Here, he told the truth. This is the flavor of the Establishment media's reviews. He then says that he told God that Americans like blood and gore.

"You listening to me, son?" God asked.

Chastened, I, said, "You're the Man."

"Who in hell, excuse my profanity, wants to sit through two hours to see a movie in Aramaic and Latin and watch my son get cut to ribbons? Son, you have better things to do. Go watch that Adam Sandler movie. It's fun and you'll love that Drew Barrymore."

Duggan then ceased any attempt to imitate Andy Rooney. He went on the offensive.

Gibson may be a wacko. He once said in an interview that "some people think I'm mad, maybe I am." And he is a Catholic conservative who hates hearing the mass in English and—God forbid—guitar playing during the service.

But he was smart enough to hire a good public relations team, and they delivered.

But Dan Klores, a very smart public relations man who has also made a finely received independent film—"The Boys of Second Street Park"—says those who engineered the publicity "ought to be ashamed of themselves."

"They have appealed to neo-fascist Holocaust deniers," Klores said. "They sold out for money. They are thoroughly cynical people."[13]

The media elite want desperately to believe that tens of millions of Americans are not committed to Jesus Christ, which includes faith in the story of His death and resurrection. They desperately want to believe that Gibson targeted his market to "neo-fascist Holocaust deniers." But, by the time Rooney read those letters to his audience, the movie had taken in well over a quarter of a billion dollars at the box office. It was not even Easter weekend yet. This must be bad news for the critics. Are there really that many neo-fascists and holocaust-deniers in America?

Paula Frederikson

In the *Christian Science Monitor*, a professor at Boston University wrote a review titled, "Controversial 'Passion' presents priceless opportunity for education: A toxic film delivers a dangerous, but teachable, moment." As they say, "the title tells all." She was one of the panelists on the ad hoc committee of Jews and Catholics to investigate the film.

> We framed our presentation by naming one precise source of concern: The long, toxic Christian tradition that Jews were—or are—particularly responsible for the death of Jesus, and how this has led to anti-Jewish violence. . . .
>
> "Passion" stands in the echo chamber of traditional Christian anti-Judaism. The tradition at its most benign has excused, and at its most malicious has occasioned, anti-Jewish violence for as long as Western culture has been Christian. . . . Christians enraged at the supposed Jewish treatment of Jesus have often acted out against Jewish neighbors in their midst, and felt morally and theologically justified in doing so.

The question facing the panel, then, was this:

> Will "Passion" have a negative effect on society? Might it promote anti-Jewish violence? I think it well might. Long cultural habits die

hard. Debate around the film has already occasioned ugly anti-Semitic slurs. My university and I have received ominous threats from a furious Christian "Passion" fan. ("I am telling you now that if this woman continues to be employed as a professor, you will be putting your university at risk.")

Let me explain to this hyperventilating academic that the phrase, "putting your university at risk," can mean putting donations at risk.

Not wanting to appear as a complete dolt, she hastened to add this:

> Will the anti-Semitism the movie has already stirred lead to violence? I think in the US it won't, despite the violence of our culture. Anti-Semitism just hasn't had the defining role here, historically, that it has had elsewhere. The long tolerance of anti-Jewish violence in Europe, and the current climate of violence against Jews—in Istanbul, South America, Britain, and France—inclines me to be much less sanguine about the effects of "Passion" there.

She might have commented on the origin of such violence in Britain, France, and Turkey. The obvious suspects are those Muslims who are committed to the Islamic tradition of violence, a tradition that brought Islamic armies to the gates of Vienna twice in early modern times. I keep wondering about what the size of the market for *The Passion* will be in radical Islamic circles. (I am not speaking here of the average Muslim, who will probably like the movie.) Why will it be so large? Maybe it will be, but those who kept repeating this refrain should have told us why.

> My point is that the toxic tradition—Jews killed Jesus; all Jews everywhere are culpable; when something bad happens to them, it is no less than they deserve—is very much alive. The film, if unaltered, is inflammatory, and potentially dangerous.
>
> My responsibility is to speak out—not against the film so much as against the ignorance and the unselfconscious anti-Judaism that it so dramatically embodies. Gibson has given us a priceless opportunity for public education. Out of the ivory tower, past the Cineplex, into

the churches and interfaith communities, this teachable moment now serves as the silver lining that shines within the looming dark cloud of Gibson's "Passion."

Well, it is always nice to know that up there in the ivory tower there are all those theological liberals who are now willing and able to go into the highways and byways of the common people to tell them about Jesus—the Jesus of their own liberal imagination. Yes, yes: I see the vision! They will go on AM radio talk shows—no, scratch that; those shows are hosted by conservatives. All right, they will go on PBS. Problem: the only time that PBS gets an audience large enough to make a difference is when they run *Antiques Road Show* or bluegrass music re-runs during fund-raising week. Well, then, what about Sunday afternoon talking head shows? Oops, sorry, that was in 1958. Today, Sunday afternoon is dominated by golf and NASCAR racing.

This lady, like most liberals, lives in the academic equivalent of the emerald city of Oz. She thinks that she and her colleagues can wage a successful war against a blockbuster toxic movie. Ho, ho, ho. And, I might add, ha, ha, ha.

Greg Easterbrook

Mr. Easterbrook writes for *The New Republic*. On his on-line forum, Easterblog, he posted his warning against *The Passion*.

> Much of the discussion over The Passion of the Christ focuses on whether it is fair to present the Jewish people or Jewish leaders of the time as the agent of Christ's death.

This statement is true. This has indeed been the focus of the Establishment media's concern, which is Abraham Foxman's concern. This is ultimately the question of whether it is fair for Bible-believing Christians to want to see on-screen what they can read in the New Testament. The author thinks that this is unfair. It turns out that we are all responsible for the crucifixion. This is a variant of the Left's refrain that we are all responsible for criminals who break the law. If he can pin the blame on everyone, a criminal can beat the rap.

> The point about theology is so simple and basic that it is in danger of being lost in The Passion of the Christ debate—and surely is lost in the movie itself. The point is that according to Christian belief, all people are equally to blame for the death of Christ, and all people are redeemed by his suffering and resurrection. Jesus' ministry and story had to happen somewhere. That it happened among Jews and Romans is no more significant than if it had happened among Turks and Persians or Slavs and Finns or any other groups. All people are equally to blame for the death of Christ, and all people are redeemed by his suffering and resurrection.

This is misleading. First, the death of Jesus came as the fulfillment of biblical prophecy. This prophecy was given to the Israelites and was regarded as authoritative by Jews in Jesus' day. The story of man from creation to the end of time is historical. There were no Finns in the Sanhedrin. Second, it is only theological liberals who believe that "all people are redeemed by his suffering and resurrection." Third, there was one man, above all men, who was responsible: Judas.

> And truly the Son of man goeth, as it was determined: but woe unto that man by whom he is betrayed (Luke 22:22)!

Helpful hint: Judas was not a Slav.

> Whether you believe these events actually happened—I do—does not matter to understanding the theological meaning of Jesus's fate, that all people are equally to blame for the death of Christ and all people are redeemed by his resurrection. The Gospels and the letters of the apostles support this conclusion; the majority of Christian commentary supports this conclusion; that all people were to blame for the death of Christ and all people are redeemed has even been the

formal position of the Catholic Church since the Council of Trent almost 500 years ago.

To say that not one word of this is true is putting it mildly. This poor soul is trying to persuade readers that his teddy bear Jesus who represents a happy face God is what the Gospels teach. It is as if Jesus' story of Lazarus and the rich man did not identify two separate non-resting places for all eternity (Luke 16). It is as if Jesus did not say:

> And fear not them which kill the body, but are not able to kill the soul: but rather fear him which is able to destroy both soul and body in hell (Matthew 10:28).

> But I will forewarn you whom ye shall fear: Fear him, which after he hath killed hath power to cast into hell; yea, I say unto you, Fear him (Luke 12:5).

Theological liberals live their lives in a make-believe world. They dismiss almost two thousand years of evidence that the vast majority of those who have called themselves Christians have not believed in theological liberalism's Jesus, a Jesus invented mainly by a handful of English deists in the seventeenth century.[14] They announce emphatically what Christianity *really* teaches, despite the fact that the creeds and councils of the church testify against them.

> The Passion of the Christ seems to urge its audience to turn away from the universal spiritual message of Jesus and toward base political anger; that is quite an accomplishment, and a deeply cynical one.[15]

Political anger. Once again, we are back to politics. This the heart, mind, and soul of liberalism, including theological liberalism.

There is a political message in *The Passion*: do not trust empire. Do not join the high priests of Jerusalem in their political confession of faith.

But they cried out, Away with him, away with him, crucify him. Pilate saith unto them, Shall I crucify your King? The chief priests answered, We have no king but Caesar (John 19:15).

Conclusion

It should be clear by now what the target of the media's attacks is: Christianity. The Jesus of the Bible they equate with the Jesus of *The Passion*. So do Christians. But there is a fundamental difference: the media elite reject the Jesus of the Bible in the name of rejecting the Jesus of *The Passion*. In doing this, they seek to undermine Christians' faith in the Jesus of the Bible.

This strategy will not work. Today, it is theological liberalism that is on life-support. *The Last Temptation of Christ* lost something in the range of $10 million, according to Michael Medved.[16] There is no telling how many hundreds of millions *The Passion* will earn.

Mel Gibson has sent the Establishment a message: there is an army of Christians out there who do not have any use for theological liberalism. Those outright atheists and secular humanists who had thought that the support of theological liberals would help them in their war against Mel Gibson now find themselves in the position of England in World War I and Germany in World War II when they put confidence in the Italian army.

Notes

1. "Maligning Mel Gibson." http://tinyurl.com/2grk5

2. James Thurber, *The Years With Ross* (Boston: Little, Brown, [1959] 2001).

3. *Dramatizing the Death of Jesus*. http://tinyurl.com/huxb

4. Eric J. Greenberg, "Gibson's 'Passion' Termed Anti-Semitic, *The Jewish Week* (June 13, 2003). http://tinyurl.com/3ygz4

5. "ADL Statement on Mel Gibson's 'The Passion'" (June 24, 2003). http://tinyurl.com/2kr6j

6. Office of Communications, United States Conference of Catholic Bishops, "Ecumenical and Interreligious Committee Responds to News Report" (June 11, 2003). http://tinyurl.com/2b88d

7. Julia Duin, "'Passion' critics retract reviews," Washington Times (Feb. 27, 2004). http://tinyurl.com/3g9kz

8. "Free Radical," *Reason* (Nov 2001). http://tinyurl.com/32gun

9. Christopher Hitchens, "I Detest This Film . . . With a Passion," The Mirror (Feb. 27, 2004). http://tinyurl.com/3604t This is a London newspaper.

10. Christopher Hitchens, "Schlock, Yes; Awe, No; Fascism, Probably," *Slate* (Feb. 27, 2004). http://tinyurl.com/2em3y

11. Andy Rooney, "As God Told Me . . ." *60 Minutes* (Feb. 22, 2004). http://tinyurl.com/37ned

12. "The Passion Over Andy Rooney," *60 Minutes* (March 14, 2004). http://tinyurl.com/208y7

13. Dennis Duggan, "A conversation with 'the Man,'" *Newsday* (Feb. 25, 2004). http://tinyurl.com/2qwa4

14. Henning Graf Reventlow, *The Authority of the Bible and the Rise of the Modern World* (London: SCM Press, [1980] 1984).

15. "Mel Gibson's Deeply Cynical Accomplishment," *New Republic Online* (Feb. 25, 2004). http://tinyurl.com/ywmxj

16. Michael Medved, *Hollywood vs. America: Popular Culture and the War on Traditional Values* (New York: HarperCollins, 1992), p. 49.

4

Is The Movie's Violence Pornographic?

All we like sheep have gone astray; we have turned every one to his own way; and the LORD hath laid on him the iniquity of us all. He was oppressed, and he was afflicted, yet he opened not his mouth: he is brought as a lamb to the slaughter, and as a sheep before her shearers is dumb, so he openeth not his mouth. He was taken from prison and from judgment: and who shall declare his generation? for he was cut off out of the land of the living: for the transgression of my people was he stricken. And he made his grave with the wicked, and with the rich in his death; because he had done no violence, neither was any deceit in his mouth. Yet it pleased the LORD to bruise him; he hath put him to grief: when thou shalt make his soul an offering for sin, he shall see his seed, he shall prolong his days, and the pleasure of the LORD shall prosper in his hand (Isaiah 53:6–10).

ISAIAH 53 IS the crucial prophecy in the Old Testament regarding the Messiah. The last day of Jesus' pre-resurrection life fulfilled this prophecy. *The Passion of the Christ* begins with a citation from this passage.

The Bible's sacrificial system, which began no later than Abel's sacrifice of an animal (Genesis 4), for which his brother Cain killed him, pointed to the shedding of blood. Even earlier, God had killed animals to provide the skins as a covering for Adam and Eve (Genesis 3). The shedding of blood is the central fact in the story of creation-Fall-redemption. The Epistle to the Hebrews says:

> But Christ being come an high priest of good things to come, by a greater and more perfect tabernacle, not made with hands, that is to say, not of this building; Neither by the blood of goats and calves, but by his own blood he entered in once into the holy place, having obtained eternal redemption for us. For if the blood of bulls and of goats, and the ashes of an heifer sprinkling the unclean, sanctifieth to the purifying of the flesh: How much more shall the blood of Christ, who through the eternal Spirit offered himself without spot to God, purge your conscience from dead works to serve the living God? And for this cause he is the mediator of the new testament, that by means of death, for the redemption of the transgressions that were under the first testament, they which are called might receive the promise of eternal inheritance. For where a testament is, there must also of necessity be the death of the testator (Hebrews 9:11–16).

The New Testament is called new because of the death of Jesus on the cross. But there was more suffering than that which was provided by the crucifixion.

> As many were astoni[sh]ed at thee; his visage was so marred more than any man, and his form more than the sons of men (Isaiah 52:14).

The cross was the judicial means of redemption for man, but the preliminary beatings provided the fulfillment of Isaiah 52:14. To leave them out of the on-screen re-creation of the crucifixion would have been a mistake. We are not provided with detailed descriptions of the beatings inflicted on Jesus by the Sanhedrin and then the Roman soldiers. We are informed by Isaiah regarding the results of these beatings.

How Much Violence in History?

The Passion has been strongly criticized for its violence. This is a strange criticism coming from liberals who have never before raised any question regarding the artistic use of violence. For a generation, violence has escalated on-screen. There have been undercurrents of criticism from conservatives and a few liberals, but these criticisms have not had a great effect in the decisions made by movie directors. The special effects departments are more noted for violence than anything else, from spattering blood to explosions. *The Wild Bunch*, Sam Peckinpah's 1969 western, drew considerable criticism from reviewers for its bloody scenes of gunfights and machine gun victims, but after that initial flurry of criticism, reviewers backed off. In the name of art, everything has been justified on-screen. Art has become the official sanctifying agency for depictions of men's more degraded practices.

The question of violence is a question of context. *Saving Private Ryan* is deservedly legendary for its re-creation of a Normandy beachhead on D-Day. Compared to *The Longest Day* (1963), it is far more accurate. It is also far more violent. Two decades ago, the late Jesse Cornish, a veteran of Normandy, described to me what he went through. He told me that some of the landing craft halted too early, and men with 80-pound backpacks jumped into water that was over their heads. They drowned. This we see on-screen. He told me that bullets killed men under water. This we also see. I read no criticism of the movie based on its violence, yet few movies ever filmed have more violence than the beachhead scenes in *Saving Private Ryan*. Why no criticism? Because the violence was not gratuitous. It was integral to Steven Spielberg's largely successful attempt to re-create the actual event. Veterans of the invasion who saw the film were stunned by its accuracy. It was what they remembered.

The Passion is a violent movie. Those who attend it know in advance that this is the case. The R-rating is surely justified. What is different about this film is the barrage of criticism from the Establishment media.

Without warning, they have abandoned the "art as sanctifying" litany and have attacked Gibson's decision to portray the violence imposed on Jesus. No other version of the crucifixion has ever approached this level of violence. The Establishment reviewers want a return to the older movies' versions.

When you see the entire media mount an assault on a lone example of on-screen violence, calling for self-restraint on the part of the director, attacking the movie as sick, or worse, because of its violence, you have grounds to suspect a hidden agenda. Something more than the reviewers' never-before offended artistic sensibilities may be at work here. This is a question of whose lamb is being gored.

> Many bulls have compassed me: strong bulls of Bashan have beset me round (Psalm 22:12).

The level of violence on-screen may be greater than what actually took place. Gibson says that he relied on an early nineteenth-century book by Anne Catherine Emmerich, *The Dolorous Passion of Our Lord Jesus Christ*, which she claimed came to her in a vision. There is no doubt that many scenes were taken from that book. Some Protestants are unhappy with the use of this source material. They believe that it adds to the New Testament's version of the story, which of course it does. This is a movie, not a documentary. But, on the whole, these criticisms have been muted. One reason for Protestant restraint is that nothing like this movie has ever been produced: a movie that puts New Testament subtitles on-screen that accurately reproduce Jesus' actual words and the words of his adversaries. Another is that Protestants know that previous Hollywood film versions have not done justice to Isaiah's account of Jesus' suffering. Third, they know that the enraged Establishment critics are most upset about those aspects of the film that are found in the New Testament's various accounts.

Protestant critics should heed the old slogan, "You can't beat something with nothing." Standing on the sidelines of culture and complaining that Catholics add too much extra stuff is not the way to pursue cultural transformation. I suspect that those Protestants who are most critical of the film are hostile to the idea of cultural transformation.

There is something else. There are anti-Catholic Protestants who are convinced that the Roman Church is still the church of the sixteenth and seventeenth centuries. They also act as though the secular humanism of our day is still the self-professed religiously neutral humanism that prevailed in the youthful America of Washington, Adams, Franklin, Madison, and Jefferson. They worry about a potential Catholic takeover of the country, but do not do anything risky or expensive to roll back the humanist takeover that was essentially complete by 1926. I noticed decades ago that spokesmen for the more sectarian and pietistic branches of Protestant fundamentalism have been unwilling to challenge the well-armed apostasy of our era, preferring instead to shadow box with enemies long since in the grave.

The scenes of the Roman soldiers beating Jesus have drawn the most criticism from reviewers, except for the movie's (New Testament's) supposed anti-Semitism. I have not seen anyone mention the following. In Latin, the soldiers count the blows. The number exceeds forty. This should draw Christians' attention back to the Mosaic law, but it won't, since so few Christians are familiar with the details of the Mosaic law.

> And it shall be, if the wicked man be worthy to be beaten, that the judge shall cause him to lie down, and to be beaten before his face, according to his fault, by a certain number. Forty stripes he may give him, and not exceed: lest, if he should exceed, and beat him above these with many stripes, then thy brother should seem vile unto thee (Deuteronomy 25:2–3).

We do not know how many stripes were inflicted, but there is no doubt that by having the soldiers count off each blow, Gibson is portraying law-breaking on a perverse scale. The soldiers were trying to make Jesus appear vile. So, from an artistic point of view, the number of wounds is on-target. That very few viewers will understand either the

Latin or the Mosaic law points to Gibson's subtlety. He paid attention to the little things.

The movie's account of the resurrection is brief. Jesus is on-screen for less than one minute. We see Him physically restored, except for a nailprint in His right hand. This is as it should be. God's judicial issue was settled by the cross, not by the preliminary beatings.

> For the preaching of the cross is to them that perish foolishness; but unto us which are saved it is the power of God (I Corinthians 1:18).

> But God forbid that I should glory, save in the cross of our Lord Jesus Christ, by whom the world is crucified unto me, and I unto the world (Galatians 6:14).

> And being found in fashion as a man, he humbled himself, and became obedient unto death, even the death of the cross (Philippians 2:8).

> Looking unto Jesus the author and finisher of our faith; who for the joy that was set before him endured the cross, despising the shame, and is set down at the right hand of the throne of God (Hebrews 12:2).

We know that He spoke with His disciples on resurrection day: the walk on the road to Emmaus and the meeting in the room (Luke 24). They did not see the signs of the beatings. But they did see the nail-pierced hands and feet.

> Behold my hands and my feet, that it is I myself: handle me, and see; for a spirit hath not flesh and bones, as ye see me have. And when he had thus spoken, he shewed them his hands and his feet (Luke 24:39–40).

In this sense, the movie is accurate. It also represents the cross as judicially central. The visible evidence of the historical event of the crucifixion remains in the resurrected body of the judicially representative agent. The lacerations do not. Put differently, the perfection of Jesus' death-free resurrected body still bore the marks of the crucifixion.

Thus, from the point of view of the theology of the event, the movie's brief resurrection scene is accurate.

The Critics' Hidden Agenda

The critics are united on the central creed of the modern West: "*There is no final judgment or hell.*" The movie teaches that Jesus experienced the judgment of men because He was experiencing the judgment of God. The offense of the gospel in our day is not that it proclaims Jesus as God. Humanists can shrug this off by saying, "Each man sees God in his own way." They cannot shrug off hell. They try, of course. They say things like this: "Some men make our own hell here on earth." But this is whistling past the fiery graveyard.

The Christian interpretation of the crucifixion is intolerable to a man in revolt against God. He is told by the creeds of the church that Jesus suffered under Pontius Pilate and was crucified. This was an historical event. Why was it necessary? What does it prove? When the humanist says that Jesus was a great teacher, but only a man, like any other man, the crucifixion becomes an example of sacrifice on behalf of your fellow man. But why was this necessary? What principle did Jesus uphold by laying down His life in this way? What was the point?

The point was, the New Testament tells us, providing a substitutionary atonement to placate a cosmically angry God.

> For scarcely for a righteous man will one die: yet peradventure for a good man some would even dare to die. But God commendeth his love toward us, in that, while we were yet sinners, Christ died for us. Much more then, being now justified by his blood, we shall be saved from wrath through him. For if, when we were enemies, we were reconciled to God by the death of his Son, much more, being reconciled, we shall be saved by his life (Romans 5:7–10).

Paul's explanation points to a God who judges. But when does God impose this wrath? And for how long? Jesus supplied the answers: (1) at the end of time (Matthew 25); (2) forever (Luke 16). Jesus, the great teacher, taught about a God who ruthlessly tortures His enemies forever.

If the critics were honest, they would not criticize Gibson for neglecting to portray Jesus as the teacher of love. They would indeed criticize him for not portraying the common sense of the Sanhedrin in getting rid of this loud-mouthed bigot, who preached the hatred of God more forcefully than anyone ever had up to that time. Jesus preached that God loves some and hates others, from start to finish. Judas is the archetype of a man hated by God.

> And truly the Son of man goeth, as it was determined: but woe unto that man by whom he is betrayed (Luke 22:22)!

Jesus said things like this:

> Think not that I am come to send peace on earth: I came not to send peace, but a sword. For I am come to set a man at variance against his father, and the daughter against her mother, and the daughter in law against her mother in law. And a man's foes shall be they of his own household (Matthew 10:34–36).

This is not the Jesus of Hollywood. Mel Gibson comes along and portrays the torture of Christ as absolutely necessary to redeem men. Redeem them from what? From hell and then, after God resurrects all men and restores perfect bodies to their souls, with which to endure even more pain, He consigns billions of them to the lake of fire. God is no teddy bear.

> And I saw a great white throne, and him that sat on it, from whose face the earth and the heaven fled away; and there was found no place for them. And I saw the dead, small and great, stand before God; and the books were opened: and another book was opened, which is the book of life: and the dead were judged out of those things which were written in the books, according to their works. And the sea gave up the dead which were in it; and death and hell delivered up the dead

which were in them: and they were judged every man according to their works. And death and hell were cast into the lake of fire. This is the second death. And whosoever was not found written in the book of life was cast into the lake of fire (Revelation 20:11–15).

The critics may not understand all of this, but they understand enough to become outraged at Gibson's portrayal of the crucifixion. They understand the question raised artistically by *The Passion*: "If God would do this to His own Son, what is He willing to do to me?" This movie proclaims graphically to millions of viewers: "If you take your stand with the Establishment and its well-paid hirelings, you will wind up in worse shape than Jesus did . . . forever." This has always been the message of the Gospel, and it has always been deeply resented by the co-conspirators.

The critics have waved the red flag of violence to persuade people that Gibson is a lover of violence, that the level of violence portrayed on-screen is not historically accurate, and even if it were, the movie would be in poor taste artistically. This is their way of saying: "Don't tell me I'm going to hell."

The Chorus of the Condemned

Some of the reviewers I refer to here are more insightful that others, but they all share the same agenda. Let us begin with one of the more insightful ones.

Kirk Honeycutt

Kirk Honeycutt's review in the *Hollywood Reporter* (Feb. 23), follows the pack by calling attention to the missing element of love, as if Jesus' submission to the crucifixion itself were not the consummate act of love in history.

Pity anyone though who comes to this movie without a knowledge of the New Testament. For them, a handful of brief flashbacks to earlier days will fail to do the trick. Yet even a Bible student might wonder why Gibson would choose to downplay the self-sacrifice and love that went into Jesus' submission to torture and death. The spiritual significance of the Crucifixion gets swamped in an orgy of violence visited upon Jesus' body. Indeed, it's doubtful any human being could remain conscious for his own execution were he to endure the level of physical abuse graphically depicted here.

By referring to the possibility that the level of abuse would have rendered Jesus unconscious, he raises a legitimate criticism. In this, he is rare among the reviewers. I had wondered the same thing as I watched the film. But his next comments reveal that he is simply a more sophisticated member of the chorus. The author is slightly better informed theologically than most of his peers: a one-eyed man in the land of the blind.

The problem with focusing narrowly on the "passion" of Christ—meaning the suffering and ultimate redemption in the final moments of Jesus' life—instead of his ministry, in which he preached love of God and mankind, is that the context for these events is lost. The Crucifixion was not only the culmination of several years of religious teachings but the fulfillment of Jesus' promise to die for the sins of mankind.

The love of God in Jesus' teachings was always contrasted to the intense hatred of God against covenant-breakers. The magnitude of God's love has meaning biblically only in light of the magnitude of God's hate. Jesus' ministry was the culmination of the teaching of the wisdom literature.

The fear of the LORD is the beginning of wisdom: a good understanding have all they that do his commandments: his praise endureth for ever (Psalm 111:10).

Surely thou wilt slay the wicked, O God: depart from me therefore, ye bloody men. For they speak against thee wickedly, and thine enemies take thy name in vain. Do not I hate them, O LORD, that hate thee? and am not I grieved with those that rise up against thee? I hate them with perfect hatred: I count them mine enemies (Psalm 139:19–22).

The fear of the LORD is the beginning of knowledge: but fools despise wisdom and instruction (Proverbs 1:7).

Honeycutt confuses metaphysics—the hidden underlying reality of the cosmos—with history. He criticizes the emphasis on the scourging. As I have already argued, this scourging had to do with the fulfillment of Isaiah's prophecy regarding the Messiah as a suffering servant. It was not an aspect of metaphysics. Honeycutt writes:

> Why do so many disciples follow this man? What does his promise of eternal life mean in the context of these events? Gibson's intense concentration on the scourging and whipping of the physical body virtually denies any metaphysical significance to the most famous half-day in history.

The crucifixion of Christ had nothing to do with metaphysics, meaning the hidden realty of nature. It had to do with justice: the need for payment to God for sin. The Fall of man was not metaphysical: a transformation of man's being. It was ethical: man's rebellion against God's law. The cross was equally ethical.

He praises the film's imagery. He ends his review with this:

> If only Gibson had chosen to highlight spiritual truth rather than physical realism.[1]

This comment indicates the degree to which the reviewer has confused spiritual with judicial. "Spiritual" without "judicial" buys you a one-way ticket on that famous road that's paved with good intentions.[2]

David Denby

Denby does what so many other reviewers do: link the agony of Jesus on-screen with Gibson's earlier movies, some of which were violent. They make it appear that Gibson's Jesus is really only Mad Max in robes.

By contrast with the dispatching of Judas, the lashing and flaying of Jesus goes on forever, prolonged by Gibson's punishing use of slow motion, sometimes with Jesus' face in the foreground, so that we can see him writhe and howl. In the climb up to Calvary, Caviezel, one eye swollen shut, his mouth open in agony, collapses repeatedly in slow motion under the weight of the Cross. Then comes the Crucifixion itself, dramatized with a curious fixation on the technical details—an arm pulled out of its socket, huge nails hammered into hands, with Caviezel jumping after each whack. At that point, I said to myself, "Mel Gibson has lost it," and I was reminded of what other writers have pointed out—that Gibson, as an actor, has been beaten, mashed, and disembowelled in many of his movies. His obsession with pain, disguised by religious feelings, has now reached a frightening apotheosis.

He understands language. He calls this a frightening "apotheosis." Synonyms include deification, exaltation, and glorification. In the context of both the review and the movie, "frightening apotheosis" is another way of saying "demonic," meaning degraded.

Not to put too fine a point to it, but when I read this, I think David Denby has lost it. "Caviezel jumping after each whack." I guess so! I mean, what did he expect? I know: Mr. Caviezel shouting in Aramaic, "Whoeee! That smarts!"

He ends his review with his secular humanist banner flying.

> The despair of the movie is hard to shrug off, and Gibson's timing couldn't be more unfortunate: another dose of death-haunted religious fanaticism is the last thing we need.[3]

Despair? For Mr. Denby and his confessional peers, the word "despair" does not come close to describing their judicial condition.

Rick Groen

This review from the Toronto *Globe and Mail*, which was posted on February 25, the day the movie opened, gives some indication of the degree of the author's commitment to the humanist agenda. He is hostile to Gibson's handling of the divinity of Jesus. I wonder: Why does an atheist care if a Christian director doesn't present Christ's divinity in a more effective way? Methinks he doth protest too much.

> Milton knew it, Michelangelo knew it, but Mel Gibson has got it ass-backwards—the rule that even artists who are inspired by their religion must still be guided by their art. So where Gibson first goes wrong in The Passion of the Christ (and he later goes badly wrong in all sorts of ham-fisted ways) is in starting with an unquestioned belief that his tragic hero is divine. Now, that belief may be a comfort to him, and to many others; properly handled, it might also make for a great film. But the handling is crucial, because art has obligations that religion does not: It must explore Christ's character, and dramatically establish both his heroism and his divinity. Neither can be assumed. If they are, if aesthetic rules get trumped by dogmatic assumptions, then what's left is not a movie but a piece of catechism. Yet that's not nearly the worst of it—in this case, the catechism is so obsessively and so graphically bloody-minded that it comes perilously close to the pornography of violence.

His phrase, "the pornography of violence," is indicative of the reviewer's antagonism to the movie, but more important, to the theological assumptions on which it rests. He continues.

> Apparently, this is a story, set in Palestine two millennia ago, that recounts the last 12 brutal hours of a convicted man's life. But who is this pathetic victim, and is there a reason to care? There isn't, because Gibson gives us none, expecting (assuming) that we'll provide our own.

By the end of the day, the movie had earned over $23 million. Apparently, a lot of people believe that there is a reason to care. But not the reviewer.

So the questions mount. Like Pier Paolo Pasolini in The Gospel According to St. Matthew, or Martin Scorsese in The Last Temptation of Christ, does Gibson try to humanize Jesus? Not really.

I deal with *The Last Temptation* in Chapter Eight. When these people say "humanize Jesus," they mean "pull him down to the ethical level of a Hollywood producer, only without the money."

He returns to the ever-popular theme of *The Passion* as a horror movie.

> Into this dramatic vacuum—Christ suffers, we suffocate—I'm pleased to report that the Devil, that old stalwart, makes several cameo appearances. Pale of countenance, blue of eye, shorn of brow, he (portrayed by a she, Rosalinda Celentano) plays a couple of Satanic party tricks and the audience—at least the horror buffs among us—couldn't be happier. Alas, his camera time is sadly limited, as Gibson insists on returning to the catechism lesson—the one that has him continually rubbing our faces in the suppurating ooze of Christ's butchered body.

There were no "party tricks." There was only the release of the snake, and Jesus' crushing of its head—as powerful an image of what the movie is all about as I could imagine.[4] But the reviewer, who I fear is representative of the theological condition of Canada, has no clue about its meaning, which is based on Genesis 3:15. He then goes on to discuss "suppurating ooze." His readers have never verbally used "suppurating" in their lives, but it sure sounds bad, doesn't it?

> The visual big top is the scourging and the crucifixion—again and again, Gibson returns to the blood-letting. Again and again, we're exposed to the clinical repetition of a single act, until an alleged act of passion comes to seem boring and passionless. Is that not a definition of pornography?

No, it is not. The word "pornography" comes from the Greek words, *pornos*, "male prostitute," and *graphos*, "writing." But this reviewer's intention is to confuse his readers and slander Mel Gibson, not inform. But he knows what Gibson has done, and he is enraged.

> But, here, his catechism is near-stupefying in its arithmetical simplicity: The greater the suffering of Christ, the greater the glory of his sacrifice, and the more graphically you depict the former, the more powerfully you imply the latter.

Well said, sir! This is correct. *The Passion* is a movie. It is made to entertain, but it is also made to convey on-screen what the New Testament teaches. But here, the reviewer refuses to adhere to the standard he laid down at the beginning, namely, that the issue is art. He is just another pagan who wants to tell Christians what their faith is all about and what they must do to defend it.

> Sorry, but the Gospels themselves—the film claims to be a compendium of the four—knew better. They all gave the blood short shrift, treating the stuff with aesthetic restraint and leaving the Church to sort out the metaphor of Communion. By contrast, like all fundamentalists, Gibson is no fan of either subtlety or metaphor—he prefers his cup of blood literal and overflowing.

This man has recognized clearly what Gibson has accomplished. The movie conveys the Gospel message to the common man better than any Hollywood film in history. It has now become a blockbuster. The cup of blood was indeed overflowing that day. The reviewer, in his utter contempt, has the story right.

> Had he not died at 33, but lived to a ripe old age and expired peacefully from a coronary occlusion, the myth would lose a bit of its redemptive power.

Indeed, it would. But now it is on-screen, and those who see it and reject it have lost any excuse on judgment day. Jesus taught:

And that servant, which knew his lord's will, and prepared not himself, neither did according to his will, shall be beaten with many stripes. But he that knew not, and did commit things worthy of stripes, shall be beaten with few stripes. For unto whomsoever much is given, of him shall be much required: and to whom men have committed much, of him they will ask the more (Luke 12:47–48).

To get the sense of rage that motivated the reviewer, read the conclusion.

Looking to heaven, Mel Gibson has made a movie about the God of Love, and produced two hours of non-stop violence. We can only pray that next time, looking to Mars, he'll make a movie about the God of Violence, and produce two hours of non-stop love. That might be porn worth paying for.[5]

Pray for this man. He needs a lot of prayer. So do his readers.

David Edelstein

This review in *Slate* (Feb. 24) does practicing Jews no good. It is as if Mr. Edelstein had read Rabbi Lapin's warning to Jews, and concluded, "I'll show Lapin a thing or two!"

He is not the only reviewer to compare *The Passion* with the *Texas Chain Saw Massacre*, but he is surely the most blatant.

You're thinking there must be something to The Passion of the Christ besides watching a man tortured to death, right? Actually, no: This is a two-hour-and-six-minute snuff movie—The Jesus Chainsaw Massacre—that thinks it's an act of faith. For Gibson, Jesus is defined not by his teachings in life—by his message of mercy, social justice, and self-abnegation, some of it rooted in the Jewish Torah, much of it defiantly personal—but by the manner of his execution.

It is always amusing to me that hard-core enemies of Christianity rush in to tell Christians what their religion is really all about. I can understand how they might tell their co-confessionalists what Christianity really means, but why do they offer me and Mel Gibson lessons in theology?

> That doesn't exactly put him outside the mainstream: The idea that Jesus died for the sins of mankind is one of the central tenets of Christian faith. But Gibson has chosen those sections of the Gospels (especially the Gospel of Matthew) that reflect the tension between Jews and Christians 50 years after the crucifixion, when the new religion's proselytizers were trying to convert, rather than incite, the Roman authorities. This is the sort of passion play that makes people mad.

So, this message makes certain people mad. Well, gosh all whillikers, I guess Christians should not make this kind of movie, or attend one when we have the opportunity, thereby encouraging its producer-director-screenwriter. Gee, I sure am glad that I now understand my responsibility. To paraphrase the opening words of *Moby Dick*, "Call me shabbos goy."[6]

> Carrying his cross, he falls again and again in slow motion on his swollen, battered body while the soundtrack reverberates with heavy, Dolby-ized thuds. It is almost a relief when the spikes are driven into his hands and feet—at least it means that his pain is almost over.
> What does this protracted exercise in sadomasochism have to do with Christian faith? I'm asking; I don't know.

Well, at least we have moved from pornography to something closer to the truth—though not much closer to the truth: sadomasochism. A sadomasochist loves pain. He loves whips. Edelstein implies that this is the force of the images on-screen. Then what of the opening scene, in the garden of Gethsemane, where Jesus prays to God that He be allowed to escape this agony—a prayer taken from the New Testament? Oops, Edelstein forgot.

> When Jesus is resurrected, his expression is hard, and, as he moves toward the entrance to his tomb, the camera lingers on a round hole in

his hand that goes all the way through. Gibson's Jesus reminded me of the Terminator—he could be the Christianator—heading out into the world to spread the bloody news. Next stop: the Crusades.[7]

Rabbi Lapin had it right.

Conclusion

The accusation that the movie is too bloody is not without merit. A Protestant director, not relying on Emmerich's account, would probably not have emphasized the beatings. But any movie that leaves Jesus' visage unmarred by beatings is inaccurate. This comment would apply to all previous Hollywood versions of the event.

There can be historical and artistic debate about how much violence was inflicted on Jesus prior to the crucifixion, but the critics have gone way beyond the category of debate. They have moved to ridicule. They are not talking about art. They are talking about the impact that this violence will have on viewers. Within the context of the subtitles, which are generally faithful to the New Testament's texts, the film's imagery brings home the central truth of the Gospel. The reviewers are not just appalled by this message of death and resurrection, of complicity and guilt. They are incensed that Gibson planned to get this message in front of tens of millions of people, and in a medium that is emotionally compelling. As it has turned out, he will probably get it in front of hundreds of millions. Maybe more. I hope so.

Notes

1. Kirk Honeycutt, "The Passion of the Christ," *Hollywood Reporter* (Feb. 23, 2004). http://tinyurl.com/2x5ba

2. To quote Steve Gillette's lyric.

3. David Denby, "Nailed," *The New Yorker* (March 1, 2004). http://tinyurl.com/2oxyy

4. It comes from Anne Catherine Emmerich's book, *The Dolorous Passion of Our Lord and Savior Jesus Christ.*

5. Rick Groen, "The Passion of the Christ," *Globe and Mail* (Feb. 25, 2004). http://tinyurl.com/33yap

6. A *shabbos goy* is a gentile who is hired by a Jew to do work that the Torah forbids, such as working on the sabbath.

7. David Edelstein, "Jesus H. Christ: *The Passion*, Mel Gibson's Bloody Mess," *Slate* (Feb. 24, 2004). http://tinyurl.com/2ht5d

Part 2

Hollywood and the
Culture War

5

The Snake in the Garden

*And I will put enmity between thee and the woman, and between thy
seed and her seed; it shall bruise thy head, and thou shalt bruise his
heel (Genesis 3:15).*

IN *THE PASSION*, the devil confronts Jesus in the garden of Gethsemane.
While there is no indication in any New Testament text that this took
place, the scene makes a powerful artistic statement. After a fruitless
attempt on the part of Satan (who is played by a woman) to persuade
Jesus that what He is about to do is impossible—bear the sins of the
world to save the souls of men—he releases a snake. Jesus is lying face-
down. He stands up. He looks down at the snake. The camera focuses
on the snake. Without warning, Jesus' sandaled foot comes down on the
snake's head. Symbolically and theologically, this is the most powerful
non-textual scene in the movie. It comes from Emmerich.

It is to Mel Gibson's lasting credit that, when the credits roll at the
end of the movie, we do not read the obligatory Hollywood statement,
"No actual snake was harmed in the making of this movie."

Gibson included this scene because it fit. It was a creative insight.
The garden of Eden is the historical and covenantal reference point:
specifically, the prediction by God, in the judgment phase of the Fall
of man, that there would be another seed, one who will crush the head

of the snake. But the snake will bruise his heel. *The Passion* is the most graphic movie ever filmed on the bruising of the promised seed's heel.

Hollywood's Garden

In modern life, the movie theater serves as a respite from the cares of the world. For a few dollars, anyone can enter a theater and be transported emotionally into a play-pretend world. The viewer leaves the world of woes for two hours, immersing himself in the cares or joys of other people. The silver screen, like some magical looking glass, allows the attendee to enter a world of image-controlled fantasy.

In the Great Depression, when the world suffered terrible economic woes, theater attendance rose to unprecedented heights. Average weekly attendance in the second half of the 1930s was over 40 percent the American population. Then came World War II. This percentage increased again, despite the fact that there were 10 million men in arms outside the country. This peaked in 1945 at 60 percent. In 1956, it was down to 30 percent. Today, it is around 10 percent, where it has been since about 1965.[1]

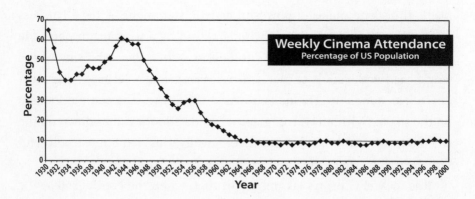

This mass-produced entertainment had no rival technologically in the 1930s and early 1940s, the era considered the golden age of the movie industry. Radio had no images. The printed word had neither sound nor images. Stage theater had always been limited to an elite. It was limited mainly to dance, music, and verbal drama. From the day in 1903 that

The Great Train Robbery opened, the movies have provided action. The model for that movie was an actual train robbery. In 1900, Butch Cassidy's Hole in the Wall Gang had stolen $5,000 (worth $100,000 today) from the Union Pacific in Wyoming. At the end, all of the movie's gang members are killed by the posse. The good guys win. Call that movie "the twelve minutes that changed the entertainment world." There had been hand-cranked peep machines with 30-second movies created by spinning photographs, but nothing like this.

That movie was filmed in New Jersey by a former employee of Thomas Edison's company. Edison had patents on movie cameras. He had created a monopoly in which his company received a percentage of the receipts from movie producers. Hollywood became the movie capital of the world from 1910 to 1918, in part because men who had seen an opportunity in the East Coast decided that patent enforcement would be more difficult in sunny California. Also, the weather allowed a longer production season. The town also had no social class structure, which for Jews who were in the process of creating the industry was an advantage. As film industry historian Neal Gabler writes, "There was no real aristocracy in place and few social impediments obstructing Jews. There was, in fact, very little of anything."[2]

The movie industry is a mass-consumption industry. Millions of people pay a little money for an hour or two of entertainment. The volume of money generated is enormous. Price competition governs the industry. It is cheaper than rival forms of equally audience-involving entertainment. Technically, a film allows great emotional involvement of the viewers, both as individuals and group members, at least in comedies. This is because laughter is contagious, especially for tightly packed audiences. The screen is so large. The images are so huge. The theater's surroundings are so dark. People's eyes are riveted to the screen, and their hearts and minds follow, at least until the experience is over.

A perennially debated question is this one: "How much longer after the experience is over?" Is it true that a movie grabs you completely, but only until you reach the parking lot? Usually, the answer is yes, but not always, and maybe not when a similar message has been presented in previous movie experiences. Movie producers who come under fire for sexually explicit or violence-filled movies usually deny that the movie experience translates into personal actions. But television advertising executives argue otherwise, at least for their own specialized applications of the fine art of movie creation.

The ethical question is a variation of the nursery rhyme: "Mary, Mary, quite contrary: How does your garden grow?" People speak of a special effects technician like George Lucas as a magician or a wizard. What do the wizards of film do with the medium? What do they plant in the garden, movie by movie?

There are patterns, surely. The movie industry thrives on knock-offs and sequels and re-makes. If the public demonstrates a pattern in preference, as revealed by ticket sales, producers will meet this measurable demand. Anyway, they will sometimes meet this demand. When there is a buck to be made, a buck will be made, other things being equal, as economists like to say. But things do not remain equal, as economists admit when pressed. Therein lies the problem, which at bottom is a religious problem, as we shall see.

Pornography and Morality

Pornography got a great boost with the invention of the camera. It takes little skill to produce pornography. There is always a market for it. Supply responds to demand, at some price. Photography lowered the price. As any economist will tell you, the lower the price, the more will be demanded.

The first great movement of pornography in the Christian West was covered up officially by the fig leaf of art. The Renaissance brought this change. The medieval world had focused on religious themes in painting. The madonna and child were universal. Anyone who doubts this should visit the largest collection of religious paintings in the world. Few people know where it is located. It is on the campus of Bob Jones University in Greenville, South Carolina. Bob Jones, Sr., toured Europe after World War II and used the university's funds to buy Europe's finest religious paintings. The collection is worth more than the campus is.

Renaissance artists celebrated the re-birth (renaissance) of classical culture. Painters and sculptures began turning to themes of classical mythology. They undressed the gods, which the Greeks also had done. In the name of art appreciation and expression, men had access to what would have been banned as pornographic prior to 1400.

Pornography invaded the movies before there were movies. The hand-cranked peep machines featured their share of topless ladies cavorting around. These ancient machines with their images of now aged or deceased "stars" were still in use in the 1950s in pre-Disney amusement parks.

Americans rarely watch silent films, other than extracts from Charlie Chaplin's comedies. So, most Americans are unaware of the existence of on-screen nudity or near-nudity prior to the enforcement of the Hays Code, also known as the Production Code, which the movie industry officially adopted in 1930, but which was not seriously enforced until mid-1934. After 1934, it was enforced voluntary by the industry for a quarter of a century. After 1960, enforcement steadily broke down. It died in 1968, after the introduction of the movie rating system.

The earliest movie that most Americans still watch for entertainment is *King Kong*, the *Star Wars* of its day. The technological marvel of stop-motion animation still amazes viewers. The fight between Kong and the tyrannosaurus rex looks as real to us as it did to our parents or grandparents. The movie was revived for theaters three times, as late as 1952, and it always did well. No other pre-*Snow White* movie ever has. Yet even here, in this action-fantasy film, we can see faint traces of the culture war: Fay Wray's diaphanous clinging gown on board the ship in the movie's account of her screen test. The scene where the ape begins to remove her clothing was cut from the 1933 release, as were the scenes of Kong trampling natives and chewing one of them. *King Kong* tiptoed around the Code.

In 1934, a hard-nosed Irish Catholic newsman Joseph Breen officially replaced the easier going Will Hays at the Studio Relations Committee, re-naming it the Production Code Administration. This had been a small committee in the Motion Picture Producers and Distributors Association (MPPDA), run by the industry. Breen had always been the power behind the throne. Now the throne had power. It wielded power because the PCA could successfully produce a movie boycott by three million Catholics who had taken a vow through the Church-related National Legion of Decency to boycott PCA-unapproved films. In the summer of 1934, Cardinal Dougherty in Philadelphia took Breen's advice and personally declared a boycott of all movie houses in Philadelphia. Attendance dropped by 15 percent to 20 percent. That same year, the National Legion of Decency was formed. Leaders in the Protestant Federal Council of Churches also threatened to organize joint protests with the Legion. This combination of events broke the film industry's foot-dragging.[3] From that point on, all scripts had to be cleared by the PCA. What the studios did not know is that a survey organized by Hays that summer discovered that the Legion of Decency had little clout. Attendance went up after a ban was declared.

Also in 1934, Clark Gable and Claudette Colbert starred in *It Happened One Night*, which won the hearts of Americans, as well as the Motion Picture Academy. It won five Oscars: best picture, best actress, best actor, best director, and best screenplay—the first picture to do so. Film buffs still watch it as a fine example of lighthearted Hollywood comedy. It was shot in 1933 and released in February. After 1934, Clark Gable would probably have been required to wear an undershirt, and there probably would not have been the "wall of Jericho" scene: a shared bedroom separated only with a vertical sheet strung up between the unmarried residents. The Code led to twin beds for married couples, as well as other inanities. This was the price that the public paid for the industry's willingness to retain common decency—rather like a safety hedge planted around a more fundamental core of moral law. It was not an excessively high price.

From the beginning, the PCA was dominated by members of the Roman Catholic Church. The Hays Code had originally been written by a priest and a layman. Yet it was self-enforced in an industry overwhelmingly dominated by Jews.[4] The story of this ethnically exclusive corporation is best told in Neal Gabler's 1988 book, *An Empire of Their Own: How the Jews Invented Hollywood*.

I do not want to give the impression that Jews did not care about the moral content of the movies. They did. But they had a public relations problem. If they exercised pressure publicly, they might fan anti-Semitism, since all but one of the studios (United Artists) in 1934 was run by a Jew or the partner of a Jew. (Daryl F. Zanuck of Twentieth-Century Fox was a Protestant. His partner was Joseph Schenck.) Felicia Herman has described the problem.

> Yet while film historians have discussed the antisemitism which often colored film reform rhetoric in this and other periods, not enough attention has been paid to the role of Jews as film reformers—not simply as the objects of reformers' ire. Indeed, in the early 1930s several Jewish organizations and individuals became deeply involved in the crusade to reform motion pictures, occupying a unique and complicated position vis-à-vis the film industry. Because there were so many Jews in Hollywood, Jewish communal leaders who might have shared the views of film reformers could not afford simply to join the crusade against "immoral" motion pictures for fear of feeding the antisemitism that drove so much of that effort. Yet neither could the Jewish community sit passively by while other groups criticized the industry, a stance that might imply either collusion with Jewish filmmakers or approval of film immorality. The explicit question became whether Jews could—and should—find a way of criticizing the product—"immoral" films—without criticizing the producer, who was so often a Jew.[5]

The head of the Anti-Defamation League, Richard Gustadt, went to Hollywood in July, 1934, to pressure Jewish executives in the industry to enforce moral standards. He met with them on the same day that the MPPDA agreed to enforce the PCA's standards. They agreed.[6] Here was a situation in which a Jewish organization whose members were middle-to-upper-class descendants of central European Jews were trying to shape the behavior of representatives of Eastern European Judaism.[7]

Did the Jews run Hollywood? Yes. Do they still? Ben Stein, the Comedy Central comedian-scholar, novelist, movie actor, columnist, and son of the Chairman of the Council of Economic Advisors under Richard Nixon, asks this question in an undated but widely quoted article: "Do Jews run Hollywood?" His answer is in the subtitle: "You bet they do—and what of it?" He says that about 60 percent of Hollywood's decision-makers are Jews. He says that Jews are "in charge" in a way that they are not in any other large business except the garment industry, scrap metal, and folding boxes. Then he names Jewish studio heads and top executives: a lengthy list. He makes an accurate point: the founders of Hollywood created "the lasting, worldwide image of America and what America is—the mass culture mirror that America likes to hold up to its face." The problem is this: when America holds up this mass culture mirror to its face these days, it gets a queasy feeling in the pit of its collective stomach.

Stein makes another crucial observation: gentiles have invaded Hollywood in the last two decades. They are bright college graduates from Harvard and similar institutions. These are the best and the brightest in America.

> The standard route to Hollywood now is through Harvard and Yale. Sitcom writers and producers, movie scriptwriters and producers now come from the Ivy League far more than from the streets of Brooklyn. Most of the writing staff of the powerhouse *Seinfeld* is from the *Harvard Lampoon*.
>
> So are many of the writers on *Married...with Children*, *Friends* and other stalwarts of the box. The route from Harvard Square to Hollywood is now hallowed by success and money. In fact, the agencies now beg and plead for *Harvard Lampoon* grads the way they once cried for the writers of *The Jack Benny Radio Program*.

Stein does not come out and explicitly say that the moral dry rot that has also appeared over the last four decades, but especially since 1980, has accompanied these highly educated gentiles. He is fully aware of the filth, and he says it appalls him. So, his two-part observation is in fact a condemnation of the output of the most prestigious institutions of higher learning in the West. He is implying, and I am saying, that moral dry rot was not invented in Hollywood; rather, it was imported from the Establishment. But Hollywood remains the foremost exporter. Cable TV is playing catch-up with Hollywood, and network TV is playing catch-up with cable.

He then asks, "Why single out Jews?" He thinks the causes are envy and anti-Semitism. This angers him. He ends the article with this challenge:

> For now, Hollywood, in many ways the most successful cultural enterprise of all time and the most potent messenger of American values of all time, is changing, but it is still largely Jewish. And a very angry voice in my curly head makes me add, "What the hell of it?"[8]

I offer another explanation for people's anger at Hollywood. Most Americans pay little attention to Hollywood's ethnic make-up. It is not Hollywood's ethnic make-up that is seen as the problem by Hollywood's growing army of critics. What offends them (us) is Hollywood's assault on traditional moral values, an agenda which rests squarely on Hollywood's religious confession: "There is, at the most, one God." It is the Ivy League's confession, too. We see the moral dry rot in the cultural mirror that Hollywood puts in front of us. It is more visible on-screen than anywhere else. There was plenty of dry rot in 1940 or 1950, but Hollywood did not hold up that mirror in front of us and say, "This is what America really is." Hollywood's Jews in 1950 were not the same as Hollywood's Jews today. Neither, for that matter, was the Ivy League.

Who Is a Jew?

This leads me to that traditional minefield question: "Who is a Jew?" This question has been a divisive factor in the Jewish community ever since the early decades of the nineteenth century, when Napoleon opened up society to Jews, who had been forced to live in walled-off urban ghettos for a millennium. It still is a divisive political issue in what Orthodox Jews[9] call the State of Israel, and non-Orthodox Jews call Israel. In the United States, there are about half a million Orthodox Jews, or about 10 percent of American Jews. Some estimates place this figure at 350,000, or 7 percent. So, in order to keep things clear for the reader, here is what the Orthodox Jew defines as a Jew. It is someone who believes in the following:

1. The Hebrew Bible is the literal word of God.
2. The first five books—the Torah—were written by Moses, who lived approximately 3,500 years ago.
3. All the books of the Hebrew Bible are binding morally and judicially: the law and the prophets.
4. The Babylonian Talmud is an authoritative compilation and commentary on the oral tradition, which stretches back to Moses.
5. The Talmud remains morally and judicially binding in the lives of Jews.
6. A literal Messiah will come to lead the people of Israel.
7. Jesus was not the Messiah.

Reform Jews (two million) share only one of these beliefs: number 7. This is mainly because they do not believe in numbers 1–6. Conservative Jews (two million), a third classification, are somewhere in between. In 1991, Daniel J. Elazar estimated that at any time, half of America's nearly six million Jews are not affiliated with the institutions of Jewish life.[10]

Reform Jews are theologically liberal. They are to Orthodox Judaism what the National Council of Churches is to fundamentalist Protestantism. Put another way: they are to Orthodox Judaism what guitar-promoting, annulment-granting American Catholicism is to Latin mass Catholics. They are the enemy.

So, when I write that Jews controlled Hollywood in the early years of the industry, and still exercise tremendous influence, which they share with banks and investment houses that finance them, I have in mind how Orthodox Jews might classify Hollywood's moguls: "Unitarians, but with better business connections." I have in mind non-practicing Jews who make it to synagogue annually (maybe) for Yom Kippur. They held fund-raisers for Bill Clinton. Milton Himmelfarb once quipped that Jews earn like Episcopalians but vote like Puerto Ricans. He was speaking of Reform Jews and non-practicing Jews.

I am aware that non-practicing Jews are slowly moving to the right politically. This fact has been revealed by a series of surveys taken by Hebrew University's Steven M. Cohen, a specialist in research on Jewish opinion. As non-practicing Jews have become assimilated into American culture, often through intermarriage, they have become more conservative politically, along with the prevailing culture. Younger Jews are more likely to vote more conservatively than older Jews. But because this political shift is in its formative stages, I have not taken it into consideration in this book.

Strange Alliances

I will take my analysis a step further. There is an operational alliance among Reform Jews, the National Council of Churches, and American Catholic bishops. It encompasses politics, but more important, it involves a shared view of the world. That view is political liberalism. It is the product of theological liberalism and too many years spent in graduate school.

In reaction to the first alliance, there has now developed another alliance. This alliance is made up of Orthodox Jews, Protestant fundamentalists and evangelicals, and socially conservative Roman Catholics, including especially Latin mass Catholics. I would date its origin with the presidency of Ronald Reagan. It has come into existence because each group has found itself under siege by the "barbarians in the gates," namely, theological liberals known collectively as the American religious Establishment. This religious Establishment has sought to speak in the name of the respective religious communions. Members in the pews or the equivalent of pews, who do not share the worldview of the religious Establishment, have begun to say, louder and louder, "They don't speak for us." I call this alliance *the disloyal opposition*.

Let me name names. Orthodox Jews: Laura Schlessinger, Rabbi Daniel Lapin, and Rabbi Lapin's better known synagogue member, Michael Medved. Protestants: James Dobson, Charles Colson, and Beverly La-

Haye. Catholics: Pat Buchanan, Phyllis Schafly, and Mel Gibson. Because Mel Gibson owns a camera and knows how to use it, he has become the most important figure in the disloyal opposition as of February, 2004. It is unlikely that he will retain this position, because he will go on to other projects, but he has become a lightning rod. His film will retain this status.

Rabbi Lapin declared in an appearance on Pat Robertson's *700 Club* that the accusation by Abraham Foxman of the Anti-Defamation League that *The Passion* is anti-Semitic puts Christians in a bind. "What he is saying is that the only way to escape the wrath of Foxman is to repudiate your faith."[11] This is indeed the problem. Because *The Passion* rests so heavily on the New Testament's accounts of what Jesus did and said, what Foxman has said about the film as anti-Semitic is a condemnation of the New Testament. It is difficult to believe that Foxman does not understand this. His target is the New Testament, but he guards himself from the charge of "anti-Christianism," which few people publicly protest any more, including most American Christians. He attacks Gibson's movie in lieu of attacking the New Testament. He has guarded himself by saying that the movie "distorts New Testament interpretation by selectively citing passages to weave a narrative that oversimplifies history, and is hostile to Jews and Judaism."[12] The question he refuses to face publicly is that so many of the subtitles are in the New Testament, and they form the basis of Foxman's accusation.

Why does Foxman care? Perhaps because he believes that millions of people who are unfamiliar with the events surrounding the crucifixion will be more affected by the movie than by the New Testament, which they have not read. Or perhaps because he cannot do anything about the New Testament. Yet, as it turned out, all he could do about *The Passion* was to give it more publicity. Like the Legion of Decency's bans after 1934, his verbal ban only increased ticket sales. He helped provide the controversy in the media that made *The Passion* a blockbuster. It was the accusation of anti-Semitism that got this movie the publicity that created the necessary "buzz" that sells tickets, especially on opening day. Gibson could not have afforded to buy the publicity that Mr. Foxman and his media allies provided free of charge.

Identifying the Snake

In 1934, there was widespread realization that the movies were moving in the direction of moral debauchery. By today's standards, the problem was minimal. But societies and civilizations move by small steps until they reach a turning point. Then they move very fast. World War I had been a turning point, and the era of the 1920s was a product of the broken social bonds of that war. The popular song, "How Ya Gonna Keep Them Down on the Farm, After They've Seen Paree?" (1919), was popular because it was recognized as true. People's loss of confidence during the Great Depression was another factor that undermined traditional morality. The rise of a separate youth culture in the second half of the 1950s—a culture that had money to spend on entertainment—was also a major transformation. Then came the Beatles and the rise of the counter-culture in 1964.

The movies moved with the drift until 1934, when there was a reversal. That reversal held firm for two decades, wavered in the mid-1950s, and collapsed after 1965.

The snake in the garden raised its ugly head about the time that Lyndon Johnson's special assistant and former advertising executive, Jack Valenti, left Washington and took over as head of the Motion Picture Association of America. That was on June 1, 1966. He ran it until one month after *The Passion* was released, when he announced his retirement.

His first major decision was to scrap the old PCA standards. He remains proud of this. "The first thing I did when I became president of the Motion Pictures Association of America was to junk the Hays Production Code, which was an anachronistic piece of censorship that we never should have put into place."[13] In 1968, the industry adopted the ratings system that still exists: G, PG (originally called M), R, and X. Valenti describes his motivation: to get in touch with the times.

By summer of 1966, the national scene was marked by insurrection on the campus, riots in the streets, rise in women's liberation, protest of the young, doubts about the institution of marriage, abandonment of old guiding slogans, and the crumbling of social traditions. It would have been foolish to believe that movies, that most creative of art forms, could have remained unaffected by the change and torment in our society.

The result of all this was the emergence of a "new kind" of American movie—frank and open, and made by filmmakers subject to very few self-imposed restraints.[14]

Conclusion

Valenti has said this about censorship. It begins with self-censorship. "When people say, I don't like that kind of film, I say, you have the most effective weapon known to man—don't go see it."[15] But he should also have expanded his assessment to include an organized boycott. If I choose not to attend, I also have the right to persuade others not to attend. Finally, there was the question of the top-down boycott: the refusal of a producer or distributor to make or show a film. That, too, is legal. Each approach deals with the snake in the garden.

In the view of some of the Hollywood elite, most of the media elite, and Abraham Foxman, *The Passion* is the snake. They did their best to stomp its head into the dust. They failed. Now they must live with the consequences. Had they said nothing, the film might have died. Had Gibson not inserted subtitles, which he initially did not want to do, he would now be a lot poorer. But the elite decided to stamp out this threat. They missed. We who support the movie watched in utter amazement when they missed. Their miss has raised a question in our minds: "How much power do they possess, really?" Whether you are Pontius Pilate or one of those studio spokesman who swore revenge against Gibson, you do not want your opponents asking this question.

Some of the tens of millions of ticket-buyers are part of the disloyal opposition. The elite want to believe that there are not many, that the movie is a fluke, that it is all a matter of entertainment. For most viewers, this assessment is correct. But social transformations are not launched by majorities. They are launched by dedicated minorities that have done their homework for a long time, and who perceive at some point that the time is right to go to the next stage of the confrontation.

We have now reached such a time.

Notes

1. Michelle Pautz, "The Decline in Average Weekly Cinema Attendance," *Issues in Political Economy*, XI (2002), graph, Appendix. http://tinyurl.com/2obqb

2. Neal Gabler, *An Empire of Their Own: How the Jews Invented Hollywood* (New York: Crown, 1988), p. 105.

3. Mark A. Vieira, *Sin in Soft Focus: Pre-Code Hollywood* (New York: Harry N. Abrams, Inc., 1999).

4. Two exceptions were Joseph P. Kennedy, the father of the future President, who gained control over RKO with his partner David Sarnoff, the founder of NBC. Kennedy had little direct influence on the industry. He was more interested in gaining access to starlets. The other gentile was Daryl F. Zanuck, who joined with Joseph Schenck in 1933 to establish Twentieth Century Pictures. The company later bought Fox Films. Not until Walt Disney produced *Snow White and the Seven Dwarfs* in 1938 did another gentile break into the guild. As a cartoonist, he was the odd man out.

5. Felicia Herman, "American Jews and the Effort to Reform Motion Pictures, 1933–1935," *American Jewish Archives Journal*, LII (2001), p. 12. http://tinyurl.com/3xv9z

6. *Ibid.*, p. 21.

7. *Ibid.*, p. 22.

8. Ben Stein, "Do Jews run Hollywood? You bet they do—and what of it?" *Eonline* (no date, but probably 1997). http://tinyurl.com/37znn This article is the top one listed on Stein's Web site: www.benstein.com/writing.html

9. The word "Orthodox" was originally used as an epithet by their liberal Jewish opponents, beginning in the mid-nineteenth century. The intellectual leader of

the Orthodox, Samson Raphael Hirsch, decided to accept the term. I. Grunfeld, "Samson Raphael Hirsch—The Man and His Mission," in *Judaism Eternal: Selected Essays from the Writings of Samson Raphael Hirsch* (London: Socino Press, 1956), p. xlvii.

10. Daniel J. Elazar, "How Strong is Orthodox Judaism—Really? The Demographics of Jewish Religious Identification," *Jewish Action* (Spring 1991). Published on-line by the Jerusalem Center for Public Affairs. http://tinyurl.com/ywct4

11. Cited by Nacha Cattan, "'Passion' Critics Endanger Jews, Angry Rabbis Claim, Attacking Groups, Foxman," *Forward* (March 5, 2004). http://tinyurl.com/3hd2f

12. "ADL Concerned Mel Gibson's 'Passion' Could Fuel Anti-Semitism if Released in Present Form" (Aug. 11, 2003). http://tinyurl.com/jpp7

13. Cited by Michael Medved, *Hollywood vs. America: Popular Culture and the War on Traditional Values* (New York: HarperCollins, 1992), p. 282.

14. Jack Valenti, "How It All Began." http://tinyurl.com/2283r

15. Cited by Medved, *op. cit.*, p. 268.

6

Hollywood's Strategy of Subversion

And Jesus said, Are ye also yet without understanding? Do not ye yet understand, that whatsoever entereth in at the mouth goeth into the belly, and is cast out into the draught? But those things which proceed out of the mouth come forth from the heart; and they defile the man. For out of the heart proceed evil thoughts, murders, adulteries, fornications, thefts, false witness, blasphemies: These are the things which defile a man: but to eat with unwashen hands defileth not a man (Matthew 15:16–20).

JESUS SAID THIS in response to the Pharisees, who had criticized His disciples for not washing their hands before eating. "Then came to Jesus scribes and Pharisees, which were of Jerusalem, saying, Why do thy disciples transgress the tradition of the elders? for they wash not their hands when they eat bread" (Matthew 15:1–2). Jesus answered that what a man is in his heart determines his status before God. There had been no command in the Old Testament regarding hand washing before meals. That requirement was part of the oral tradition. Jesus did not regard the oral tradition as binding.

This perception of causation—from heart to behavior—applies also to culture. What a society or a group does should be consistent to what its members believe. Men must work out their view of salvation with fear and trembling (Philippians 2:12). The visible practices of a culture come from its first principles. Therefore, any successful transformation of a society must begin in the heart, meaning men's faith in the way the world works. Men must believe that right makes might, that obedience to a set of fixed moral principles brings success in this life and the life beyond. They must believe, as Moses believed,

> And it shall come to pass, if thou shalt hearken diligently unto the voice of the LORD thy God, to observe and to do all his commandments which I command thee this day, that the LORD thy God will set thee on high above all nations of the earth: And all these blessings shall come on thee, and overtake thee, if thou shalt hearken unto the voice of the LORD thy God (Deuteronomy 28:1–2).

In other words, obedience is an outworking of faith. If a society loses faith in the legitimacy of its religious and ethical principles, its obedience will weaken. This will eventually produce a disaster. Again, quoting Moses:

> And it shall be, if thou do at all forget the LORD thy God, and walk after other gods, and serve them, and worship them, I testify against you this day that ye shall surely perish. As the nations which the LORD destroyeth before your face, so shall ye perish; because ye would not be obedient unto the voice of the LORD your God (Deuteronomy 8:19–20).

Keep this in mind whenever you read about the culture war. We are in a war for the hearts and minds of men. *The Passion* has served as a kind of hunting dog. It has flushed a lot of quail out of hiding. But this culture war began a long time ago. It began in the garden of Eden.

I do not plan to offer a history of the culture war from Eden to the present. But you need to know something about the culture war over the last three generations. So, permit me to present a quick survey of the war that we in the West think we won, fair and square, in 1991: the war against Communism. Did we win it or not?

Marxism and Culture

Karl Marx (1818–1883) was the founder of Communism. He was a materialist and an atheist. He was not a proletarian. He was the son of a successful lawyer, who had officially converted to Christianity. Marx in his youth was a professed Christian. He wrote a student paper in which he declared that "Deity never leaves mortal man wholly without a guide; he speaks softly but with certainty."[1] He did not remain a Christian after his first months at the University of Berlin. He spent most of his retirement years in considerable wealth due to support from his partner, Frederick Engels, the owner of a successful textile firm. Marx's income after 1869 put him in the upper two percent of income-recipients in England, the richest nation on earth.[2] His poverty before 1869 was due to the fact that he would not go out and get a job. He was neither a proletarian nor a member of the bourgeoisie. He was a moocher.

One of his most influential ideas was that the mode of production in a society determines the economic classes of society. The economic needs of each class in turn determine its ethics and philosophy. There is no universal morality, he taught. There is only class morality. Marx taught that the superstructure of a society—its ideas, morals, and religion—are determined by its substructure: the mode of production. Each stage of civilization reflects the existing mode of production. The superstructure of culture is derivative. It comes from the economic needs of the ruling class, which is defined economically.

Marx had a major problem with his thesis: he never defined "class." He became a Communist in 1844. He wrote continuously for the public until the late 1870s—book shelves of material. Yet he never defined "class." In the final chapter of the unpublished third volume of his most famous book, *Das Kapital* (*Capital*), he wrote: "The first question to be answered is this: What constitutes a class?"[3] Three paragraphs later, the book ends. He lived another fifteen years. He never got back to it.

The Marxists' theoretical problem in the twentieth century was this: the revolution that Marx predicted had to come in the most economically developed societies. It never did. It came in Russia, which was the most economically backward of the great European powers in 1917.

Gramsci's Revision

This fact bothered an Italian Communist, Antonio Gramsci, who not only saw the Russian Revolution, he left Italy in 1922 to journey to Russia as a delegate to the Communist International. He spent eighteen months there. He returned to Italy in late 1923. He was elected to Italy's Chamber of Deputies in 1924. In 1926, he was arrested and sent to prison, where he remained until his death in 1937. There, he wrote what became known as his prison writings.

There was a related theoretical problem. The workers of Europe had supported the capitalist powers' war in 1914. Why? The war was not in their class interest. Marxists and socialists had said this right up until the war broke out. As soon as the war began, the workers in each country supported their nation. Why was it that the proletarians had thought and fought just like everyone else? Where was the class consciousness that Marx had said must exist? If it was not there, how could capitalism ever be overthrown?

Gramsci searched for a theoretical explanation that was consistent with Marx's theory of class revolution. He never discovered it. What he offered as a modification of Marx's theory of economic determinism was in fact a repudiation of that theory. In his prison notebooks, he sketched a theory of culture and society and their relation to Communist revolution. He argued that European proletarians had adopted a bourgeois outlook. The West was inherently Christian, and the culture of Europe reflected this. The materialism of Marxism could not penetrate the typical proletarian because he was too much a product of an alien culture, i.e., Christianity. There would be no Communist revolution until the proletarians developed a uniquely proletarian way of looking at the world. How can this happen? They must first lose faith in the bourgeois capitalist outlook. But how can this ever happen? It will happen when most of the bourgeoisie also lose faith in its own world-view. By undermining the bourgeoisie's confidence in its worldview, the Communist intellectual can advance the revolution.

This added a new arena of class conflict to the Marxist program of subversion. It carried the conflict into culture in the broadest sense. The Communist Party would have to stop devoting all of its resources to organizing cells in the labor union movement. It would have to create a termite strategy in order to undermine the foundation of bourgeois society: its culture. In 1921, before he went to Moscow, he outlined his strategy.

> Nothing in this field is forseeable except for this general hypothesis: there will be a proletarian culture (a civilization) totally different from the bourgeois one and in this field too class distinctions will be shattered. Bourgeois careerism will be shattered and there will be a poetry, a novel, a theatre, a moral code, a language, a painting and a music peculiar to proletarian civilization, the flowering and ornament of proletarian social organization. What remains to be done? Nothing other than to destroy the present form of civilization. In this field, 'to destroy' does not mean the same as in the economic field. It does not mean to deprive humanity of the material products that it needs to subsist and develop. It means to destroy spiritual hierarchies, prejudices, idols and ossified traditions.[4]

This was not Marxism. It placed far too much emphasis on what Marx had called the superstructure: ideas and culture. Until the mode of production shifted to socialism, Marx had taught, there could be no creation of the final Communist paradise. In contrast, Gramsci taught that until bourgeois society loses faith in the superstructure—religion, philosophy, and culture—the Communist revolution would not occur in the West.

Malachi Martin was a conservative Roman Catholic scholar who explained Gramsci's strategy in his book on Pope John Paul II, *The Keys of this Blood* (1990).[5] He explained Gramsci's problem.

Gramsci agreed that the great mass of the world's population was made up of workers. That much was plain fact. What became clear to him, however, was that nowhere—especially not in Christian Europe—did the workers of the world see themselves as separated from the ruling classes by an ideological chasm.

And if that was true, Gramsci argued, then Marx and Lenin had to be wrong in another of their fundamental assumptions: There would never be a glorious uprising of the proletariat. There would be no Marxist-inspired overthrow of the ruling "superstructure" by the working "underclasses." Because no matter how oppressed they might be, the "structure" of the working classes was defined not by their misery or their oppression but by their Christian faith and their Christian culture.[6]

. . . If there was any true superstructure that had to be eliminated, it was the Christianity that had created and still pervaded Western culture in all its forms, activities and expressions.[7]

Gramsci's answer was therefore to wage a war against Christian culture. To be successful, this war had to be conducted anonymously. It would have to be in the name of mankind's liberation—throwing off the repressive shackles of bourgeois Christian culture. Martin comments:

It was also obvious that such goals, like most of Gramsci's blueprint, had to be pursued by means of a quiet and anonymous revolution. No armed and bloody uprisings would do it. No bellicose confrontations would win the day. Rather, everything must be done in the name of man's dignity and rights, and in the name of his autonomy and freedom. From the claims and constraints of Christianity, above all.[8]

We have seen the collapse of Communism in our day, but we have not seen the collapse of Gramsci's vision. The culture war that is going on all around us is consistent with Gramsci's description of a workable program of revolution.

I am not arguing that Gramsci's case for Communism was any better than Marx's was. Communism is an economic failure. It does not work. The East Germans tried to make it work, and they couldn't. If the Germans could not make it work, it will not work. I am saying something more relevant. Gramsci's vision of culture as the battleground for revolution—any revolution—is correct. It is not the mode of production that creates revolutions. It is intellectuals like Marx and Gramsci who create the initial vision of the revolution. Then ruthless men like Lenin or Hitler or Mao or Pol Pot organize conspiratorial groups that become successful when there is a military, social, political, or economic crisis.

Creating a positive vision of the coming paradise is not enough to produce a revolution. The intellectuals have another task: to undermine men's faith in the existing social order. Revolutionary intellectuals must work to undermine other intellectuals' faith in the legitimacy of the prevailing social order. These converts then spread despair and dissatisfaction to those lower down on the hierarchy of influence. The revolutionary intellectuals do not need to convert other intellectuals to a specific program or revolutionary theory. They need only undermine those other intellectuals' faith in the existing social order. This means that the revolutionaries must undermine men's faith in the existing social order's morality and, ultimately, its religion.

Mikhail Gorbachev has never officially abandoned his faith in Communism. On the contrary, he has consistently maintained that he is still a Communist. He is widely quoted as follows: "The market is not an invention of capitalism. It has existed for centuries. It is an invention of civilization." There is no question about this fact: Marx never taught such a doctrine. There is also no question that this view is quite consistent with Gramsci's.[9] To the extent that Marxists have adopted Gramsci's version of Marxism, the war is not yet won.

Here is my point. *If you want to orchestrate a revolution, you must first undermine men's confidence in the existing civilization.* To do this, you must undermine their faith in the religious principles that are the true substructure of civilization. Marx was wrong about both the source of the social revolution—the mode of production—and therefore the way to foment revolution. Gramsci was right.

The world is not going to get a Leninist revolution. That deeply religious worldview cost at least a 100 million lives in the twentieth century.[10] This estimate does not count an additional 40 to 50 million people who died in World War II, which was the product of Hitler's millennial vision of a thousand-year reich, which was reacting against Lenin's millennial vision of the Marxist utopia. This was a terrible price to pay to prove that Communism does not work. But it is now a visible dead end.

The problem today is this: those committed revolutionaries who favored Gramsci's version of Marxist revolution did superb work in recruiting and training the termites of the existing culture. The West's superstructure is now seriously weakened. For three generations, Gramscian Marxists recruited intellectuals and artists, who in turn began the work of undermining Western civilization. The termites have multiplied. The structure has holes in it. What now? Is there too much rotten wood for the system to remain standing?

Gramsci and Rome

Martin was convinced that Pope Paul VI had done Gramsci's work for him at Vatican II by re-focusing the work of the Church on social reform at the expense of spiritual regeneration. The Church must serve men's needs, Paul VI had told the departing bishops. This, Martin argued, was a program to secularize the Roman Church.[11] It took less than a decade for this secularization process to capture the Roman Church. On this point, the former theologically and politically conservative Catholic, who is today a liberal/radical Catholic, columnist Garry Wills, agrees with Martin. His 1972 book, *Bare Ruined Choirs*, discussed in detail the transformation of the American Roman Church after Vatican II, which had taken less than a decade. Martin, in his book, *The Jesuits* (1987), surveys the specifics of this transformation with respect to that ancient order. He subtitled his book, *The Society of Jesus and the Be-*

trayal of the Roman Catholic Church. He knew. He had been a Jesuit, and had been granted a papal dispensation to escape his vows.

There is no doubt that Mel Gibson has abandoned the post-Vatican II legacy of the Church. There is also no doubt that the spiritual heirs of Gramsci in Hollywood and the media understand that *The Passion* is Gibson's self-conscious attempt to call his church back to its pre-Vatican II roots. They hate him for this, and they have said so again and again.

The literally overnight success of *The Passion* indicates that there is more good wood remaining in Western culture, at least in the United States, than the vociferous critics of the movie think. This infuriates them. They recognize the enemy. Gibson has revealed just how much work the spiritual heirs of Gramsci have ahead of them.

Undermining a Culture

Beginning in 1966, the movies became the first mass-medium to abandon standards of moral and verbal propriety that had governed Western culture since the fall of Rome. Rome had been debauched. Augustine in his masterpiece, *The City of God*, written four centuries after the crucifixion, surveys the debauchery of Rome, which had become debauched before Jesus' era. In Book II, he makes his case against the immorality of pagan Rome. The gods of the classical world were immoral. So were local gods. In his youth, he had seen plays performed for the Berecynthia (Cybele), the mother of all the gods. "And on the holy day consecrated to her purification, there were sung before her couch productions so obscene and filthy for the ear—I do not say of the mother of the gods, but of the mother of any senator or honest man—nay, so impure, that not even the mother of the foul-mouthed players themselves could have formed one of the audience. . . . If these are sacred rites, what is sacrilege?"[12] It was only in his lifetime that the murderous games of the Colosseum were finally stamped out by the emperor, three generations after Constantine had converted to Christianity. In the fringe areas of the Roman Empire, the games went on until the barbarians conquered a region and banned them.

When Jack Valenti scrapped the Production Code in 1966, there were no longer any standards to enforce, other than those which would bring a movie or a local theater manager under local prosecutors for pornography. The courts had steadily ceased prosecuting pornography after *Playboy* survived the first tests, a decade before Valenti took over at the Motion Pictures Association of America. To make the legal case for on-screen pornography, the industry only had to segregate the audiences by age. Here was the logic: "If a still photo was legal in a magazine for sale only to adults, then a moving image was legal in an adults-only theater." Then Hollywood learned that X-rated, adults-only films did not sell. The R-rated films were adults-mainly: soft-core pornography. This process was accelerated by the advent of the multi-screen movie theater, which began to replace single-screen theaters in the mid-1960s. Now, one screen/room could be segregated for an adults-mainly picture. The theater complex retained its status as a family theater. Then it became an "entertainment complex."

The MPAA issued the new standards in 1968. From then on, consumer preference would rule. That, at least, was the economic theory, a theory based on Adam Smith's *Wealth of Nations*. Even the most politically liberal of Hollywood's personalties were vocal defenders of the principle of consumer authority in the area of movie attendance.

The free market economic theory teaches two principles of authority: (1) legal authority over property; (2) economic authority by consumers. Consumers possess the most marketable commodity: money. It takes no creativity to "sell" money. People line up to take it from us. It takes creativity to sell everything else. So, the consumer who possesses money is the last person in the long chain of exchange. He has economic clout.

The product owner does not have to sell what he owns. He may not have much economic authority, but he does have legal authority. If consumers want one item, and a seller has another item to sell, the seller is not going to make a sale unless he lowers his price. But he nevertheless retains the legal right not to sell whatever it is that he owns. In other words, if he is willing to take a chance, he can continue to offer whatever it is that he has to sell at a price that no consumer is willing to pay.

We may think of Hollywood as money-driven. If we do, we do not do justice to Hollywood. Everyone wants to make more money, *other things being equal*. But in Hollywood, other things are rarely equal.

Medved's Complaint

Michael Medved for twelve years was the co-host of the PBS show, *Sneak Preview*. He was also a screenwriter. He now is a talk-show host, a career that does not require him to immerse himself in big screen assaults on biblical morality.

In his 1992 book, *Hollywood vs. America*, he offers a history of the moral decline of Hollywood's movies. In a TV documentary that he produced, he argues that the decline began in 1960, the year that *Ben-Hur* won eleven Oscars. It began with *Inherit the Wind*. I discussed this thesis in the Introduction.

He begins his book, even before the table of contents, with a quotation from the legendary director, Frank Capra, who is most famous for Jimmy Stewart's most beloved movie, *It's a Wonderful Life*. He also had a string of hits in the 1930s, including *It Happened One Night* (1934), which was the first film to win five academy awards: "a clean sweep." Capra eventually quit Hollywood in disgust, and then wrote an autobiography that included an attack on the moral debauchery of the film industry. Medved regards these words as crucial for laying the groundwork for his book:

> Only the morally courageous are worthy of speaking to their fellow men for two hours in the dark. And only the artistically incorrupt will earn and keep the public's trust.

Part I of Medved's book is titled, "The Poison Factory." Chapter 1 is titled, "A Sickness in the Soul." Chapter 2: "A Bias for the Bizarre." Then comes Part II: "The Attack on Religion." Part III: "The Attack on the Family." Part IV: "The Glorification of Ugliness." You get the general idea. On the opening page, he writes a memorable sentence: "The dream factory has become the poison factory."

Medved takes the same approach that I do in this book, and for the same reason: we are both theists. We also believe that there is an inseparable link between religion and culture. He sees the movies as one segment of culture in the broadest sense. So do I. He offers Americans a warning: we do not understand the nature of the culture war. This is why we are losing it.

> One of the symptoms of the corruption and collapse of our popular culture is the insistence that we examine only the surface of any piece of art or entertainment. The politically correct, properly liberal notion is that we should never dig deeper—to consider whether a given work is true, or good, or spiritually nourishing—or to evaluate its impact on society at large. We routinely focus on superficial skill and slick salesmanship, while ignoring the more important issues of soul and substance. In the process, we have abandoned traditional measures of beauty and worth, accepting the ability to shock as a replacement for the old ability to inspire.[13]

The Attack on Morality

The ratings system allowed producers, distributors, and theater owners to restrict censorship by local governments. The Supreme Court had steadily tied the hands of the civil government's censors, first in literature in the 1950s, then in magazines, then on-screen. As for fine arts, they had been freed up in the fifteenth century.

By the time the new code was installed, movie attendance had fallen to 10 percent of the population attending a movie weekly. The long slide hit bottom, where it has stayed. Nothing the industry has done since then has had any positive effect on attendance.

Hollywood had a free reign after 1968. The counter-culture which had appeared in full force no later than 1965 was unstoppable. In every area of life, experimentation became the order of the day. But the process of rapid cultural revolution was set back on May, 4, 1970, at Kent

State University. When the National Guard shot and killed four students, the campus revolution ceased. Nixon had announced the invasion of Cambodia on April 30. Radical students vowed to protest when they returned in the fall semester, but they didn't. In the fall of 1970, when students returned to campus, the mood had changed. A recession had hit, and job opportunities for graduates shrank rapidly. The campus revolution, begun at Berkeley in 1964, ended. It never returned.

Nevertheless, the Establishment could not go back to the pre-1964 era. No one could. So, the familiar process of co-option, absorption, and accommodation began. Every institution bent. The process of cultural transformation did not stop, but from that time on, the revolutionaries would make progress slowly. A decade later, Ronald Reagan was elected, and conservatives began resisting more effectively. But no one, least of all Reagan, suggested that the good old days could be recovered.

Hollywood is constrained by vision at the top and ticket sales at the bottom. The old Hollywood was dead. The Justice Department had broken the legal link between production and theater distribution. That broke the back of the studio system. It transferred power to those producers who could fund new projects. New York bankers became more powerful than ever. Hollywood ceased to be a company town. This was a long time coming.

To get back the lost audience, a new breed of producers began listening to directors who promised big changes. The old ways had failed. The audience was gone. Something had to be done. No one knew what. That opened a window of opportunity to cultural radicals. What took place on the campus also took place in Hollywood. As dorms were becoming co-ed on campus, films were losing discretion on-screen. By 1980, the process was complete in both institutions. America was not the same society it had been before the moral erosion process began. Neither was its culture. Hollywood has shown the difference in the original *Back to the Future* (1985). The movie ends with the mother encouraging her son to spend the weekend alone with his girlfriend. That was the new Hollywood speaking. The fact that viewers barely noticed indicates just how well Hollywood has done its work.

The movies did not cause the sexual revolution or any other revolution, but they have reinforced these revolutions. The movies have publicly tested the limits of public tolerance of the new morality, which is the old immorality. Again and again, Hollywood has lost money on these R-rated experiments, as Medved shows. But the industry has kept trying, despite the poor box office results. It is not that Hollywood is filled with reds. It is that Hollywood is filled with red ink. The moguls, such as they are these days, have not discovered a way to increase profits and still retain allegiance to the Code, meaning the Cole Porter Code: anything goes.

Hollywood tells us that meaningful movies should deal with the real world. This is a lie. When was the last time you saw a movie in which a family (1) goes to church weekly and (2) watches seven hours of TV a day? The next time will be the first. But the best answer I ever heard to the comment, "art should deal with reality," was on-screen. It was in the Neil Simon play/movie, *Butterflies Are Free*. The blind hero, who hopes to become a writer, wants to know his writer-mother's opinion of a play. She did not like it, she tells him. It was disgusting. (I am going by a 30-year memory, so don't hold me to details.) The mother was played by Eileen Heckert, one of the most underrated actresses in American film history. He responds that plays should deal with real life. Her answer was perfect: "Diarrhea is also part of real life, but I don't want to see it on stage."

At the peak of the counter-culture, 1969, Gunther Stent, a microbiologist, wrote a little book that few people ever read. It was called *The Coming Golden Age: A View of the End of Progress*. I will not pretend that I understood then or now recall anything in his chapter on microbiology. But his book's primary thesis has remained with me. He argued that with every revolution in culture, the result is more anarchy. A scientist might call this process cultural entropy: the dissipation of energy and an increase in randomness. A good scientist wouldn't call it this, but non-scientific authors might, and have.[14]

Stent argued that with each rejection of prevailing standards, it becomes less and less possible to make the next advance. With fewer and fewer standards to revolt against, each new move is less coherent. Marlon Brando's famous response in *The Wild One* (1953) comes to mind. When a girl sees the letters BRMC on the back of Brando's motorcycle jacket, she asks him what the letters stand for. Answer: Black Rebels Motorcycle Club. She then asks, "What are you rebelling against?" He replies, "What have you got?" That quip seemed clever to my generation until we reached adulthood. Then it seemed naive.

Here is the revolutionary's inescapable problem: when there is nothing remaining to rebel against, because all restrictions have been abolished by previous revolutions, how will anyone be able to assess either the direction or creativity of the next recommended change? Chaos and incoherence will triumph.

Medved has a chapter on the foul language of the movies. What he does not mention is that foul language no longer shocks. This is always true of dirty words. They are employed, creatively and uncreatively, to emphasize a point or to shock. But they lose their power when they become common. Bad language is self-defeating when it becomes widespread.

So does nudity on-screen. So do ugliness, violence, and computer-generated special effects. Compare the first two *Star Wars* movies with the last two. The latest special effects are amazing, but they do not compensate for the sub-standard dialogue and plots.

This is Satan's permanent problem in history. He is not the Creator. He is, at best, re-creative. The more he seeks to become creative by abandoning God, the less effective he becomes. This is equally true of his earthly disciples. The quest for total autonomy brings loneliness. The quest for total perfection brings despair. The quest for total power brings intrigue, revolts, and assassinations. Satan has the reverse Midas touch.

In the early stages of any successful cultural breakthrough, the pioneers seem creative. But if they rely on an assault against permanent moral standards, the revolution will dissipate. Think of the Beatles in 1966: the *Revolver* album. Then consider what happened to the quality of their output. First the Beatles, then the Rolling Stones. Then came KISS—arguably the smartest guys in show business history: universally recognized on stage, but when they took off their make-up, they could go anywhere and not be hounded by fans or autograph seekers. After KISS, it got really bad. This process of decline is as true of Renaissance art as it is of the movies. *Bonnie and Clyde* seemed ever so creative in 1968. Who watches it today? Who watches the uncreative imitations that followed? But people still watch *Casablanca* and *It's a Wonderful Life* and *Shane*. The basics still have a market.

The Attack on Religion

In Chapter 4, "Comic Book Clergy," Medved contrasts the movies of an earlier generation with recent films. There was *Going My Way*, which won Bing Crosby an Oscar for his role as a priest. There was *The Bells of St. Mary's*, another Crosby hit, in which he played a priest. There was Spencer Tracy in *Boys' Town*. Pat O'Brien starred in *Angels With Dirty Faces* and *The Fighting 69th*. Then came the decline, beginning in the 1970s but escalating in the 1980s.[15] Noted director Stanley Kramer (*Inherit the Wind*) gave us a turkey, as Medved calls it, *The Runner Stumbles*. So few people saw it that it cannot be fairly described as forgotten. Dick Van Dyke, the famous comedian, plays a priest who falls in love with a woman and then murders her. A barrel of laughs, no doubt. *Monsignor* starred Christopher Reeve as a totally corrupt priest. He cooperates with the Mafia. *Agnes of God* shows a nun who gives birth and then flushes the baby down a toilet. Her mother superior wants to cover up the crime. Hiring the great actress Anne Bancroft, the wife of Jewish comedian Mel Brooks, to play the mother superior is not what I would call "sensitive," let alone sensible. However, if the director was trying to fan the flames of anti-Semitism, this casting strategy was right on-target. *Heaven Help Us* got no help at the box office. It was a comedy about a group of stupid priests in a parochial school who tried to control lovable, raunchy, teenage boys. *Last Rites* was the story of a priest, son of a Mafioso, who falls in love with a woman and is entangled with the mob and murder. *We're No Angels* squandered the talent of Robert De Niro. He and Sean Penn play escaped prisoners who pretend to be priests. They are honored as distinguished scholars by members of a religious order. *Nuns on the Run* "starred" two obscure British actors playing small-time gangsters who dress up as nuns and hide out in a convent. This sisters act bombed at the box office. *The Pope Must Die!* has the Pope surrounded by sultry nuns serving as his harem. Most of these movies you did not hear about. The only one you did hear about was *Godfather III*, which has Michael Corleone buying the support of the Vatican, whose officials know who he is and what he has done.

Hollywood is an equal opportunity subverter. The Protestants got their turn.[16] *Crimes of Passion* starred Anthony Perkins as a skid row evangelist who enjoys peep shows. He tries to murder a prostitute. *Children of the Corn* shows a group of religious teenagers killing their parents and taking over an Iowa town. They follow a wild Pentecostal preacher. *The Vision* has Christians using hypnotic TV technology to take over the world. This plot line does not ring true—not because TV is not near-hypnotic, but because Christians never make it onto the networks. *Light of Day* was directed by Paul Schrader, screenwriter for *The Last Temptation of Christ*, who is the most culturally influential ex-member of the Christian Reformed Church. The movie tried to bring an audience into the theater with a story about a midwestern minister who seduces a teenager and fathers a baby. Then he denounces her as immoral. The audience did not show up. *Pass the Ammo!* was a thinly veiled spoof based on TV talk-show host Jim Bakker, who was hit by a sex scandal. *The Handmaiden's Tale* starred Robert Duvall and Aiden Quinn. It is the story of what would happen if fundamentalist Christians ever do take over the country. They enslave all women. (The screenplay was clearly not written by anyone who has dealt with wives of Southern Baptist deacons.) *The Rapture* tells the story of a woman who joins a church, decides that Jesus is coming again soon, and takes her young daughter into the desert to meet Him. When He does not show up, she shoots her daughter. Medved describes the church:

> Throughout the film, Christian believers are portrayed as twitching zombies, with an obvious edge of madness behind their fervent beliefs. The only church you ever see in the film is a cultish congregation of about a dozen leisure-suited losers who worship an eleven-year-old

African-American "prophet" who barks out weird metaphysical commands like a pint-sized Jim Jones.

At the end of the film, the woman announces, "You're supposed to love God no matter what. But I *don't* love Him anymore. He has too many rules."[17]

Movies demeaning rabbis occasionally appear, as Medved shows.[18] I do not recall, nor does Medved mention, a single movie about either a corrupt or buffoonish synagogue. We Christians do eventually figure out who the targets are.

I deal with Hollywood's archetypal attack on Christianity, *The Last Temptation of Christ*, in Chapter Eight.

Not for Money's Sake Alone

Medved reveals something that most people do not know and would not guess: G and PG movies consistently make more money than R-rated movies. He titles the chapter, "Motivations for Madness." He writes:

> Looking over *Variety*'s list of top 10 box-office films of the decade of the 1980s, only one—*Beverly Hills Cop*—happened to be rated "R," even though "R" films accounted for more than 60 percent of all titles released in this period.
>
> At the same time, "PG," films represented less than 25 percent of all titles—but occupied *six* of the top 10 places on the list of the decades leading money-makers.
>
> If you expand calculations to consider the twenty leading titles in terms of box-office returns between 1981 and 1990, 55 percent were rated "G" or "PG"; only 25 percent were "R" films.
>
> An analysis of all 1,010 domestic releases logged into the comprehensive data base at Robert Cain Consulting Associates between 1983 and 1989 demonstrates a dramatic and unmistakable public preference for family-oriented material. During this period, all "G" films achieved a median box office gross of $17.3 million, while "PG" titles earned a median figure of $13.0 million. For "PG-13" releases, the numbers

dipped sharply to $9.3 million, while "R" pictures returned an even more median gross of $8.3 million.

He then cites the figures for 1990. That year, Hollywood produced four time as many "R" titles as "G" and "PG" combined: 64 percent to 14 percent. Results: the annual top 20 included the same number (seven) of "PG" and "R" titles.[19] He then draws the conclusion, in italics: "*Taken together, the numbers since 1980 show that a given "G" or "PG" film is nearly five times more likely to place among the year's box-office leaders than an "R" film.*"[20] When challenged by one Hollywood insider to show that this pattern was true for all films, not just top performers, Medved went to the Director of Research for the Screen Actors Guild, the actors' union, Robert D. Cain. Cain analyzed 221 films in 1991, which covered most of Hollywood's annual output. Here is his assessment:

> . . . By almost every measure, "R"-rated films are less likely to succeed at the box office than their "G," "PG," and "PG-13" counterparts. R-rated films generate substantially less revenue, return less profit, and are more likely to "flop" than films aimed at teen and family audiences.[21]

It gets even more amazing. An R-rated film generated less than $2 million in 41 percent of the cases. This dismal result occurred in only 28 percent of PG films. Thirty-eight percent of PG films exceeded $25 million, but only 19 percent of R-rated films did. In 1991, the median PG-rated film grossed $15.7 million, almost triple the median R-rated film's receipts of $5.5 million.[22]

These figures make one thing perfectly clear: *Hollywood is driven by something in addition to money.* Medved says what this is: "The Hollywood community wants respect even more than it wants riches; above all, its members crave acceptance and recognition as serious artists. Money is not the main motivation for their current madness."[23]

If you want to be given something, then someone or something must give it. You are therefore subordinated to that person or thing. So, we must ask this question: "Who gives Hollywood's decision-makers the respect they crave?" Surely, it is not viewers. The viewers keep sending Hollywood a message: "*Give us family-based entertainment.*" Hollywood keeps ignoring the message. The viewers send this message in the free market's way: wrapped in money. This does little good.

The Jewish moguls who ran Hollywood in the 1930s also wanted social acceptance, but they wanted money first. They made films for the family. They catered to gentile tastes, and tens of millions of the gentiles reciprocated by sending them money, week after week, even during the Great Depression. This was a mutually beneficial relationship, and it worked well, most of the time, for a quarter century. The founding moguls were Republicans, except for the Warner brothers in the early 1930s. Even they returned to the Republican fold by 1936.[24] Yet their movies were aimed at Democrats, who were the majority.

What we have seen is the devolution of Hollywood's on-screen morality. This devolution has been a universal phenomenon. It has affected every institution, including the church. Surely, it has affected the educational system. We have seen the reversal of traditional standards, which were mainly Christian standards. This is common in periods of moral decline. This was also the moral condition of Judah in Isaiah's day, which is why he offered this prophecy of hope:

> The vile person shall be no more called liberal, nor the churl said to be bountiful (Isaiah 32:5).

The politically and theologically liberal churls in the media have even reversed the meaning of the word "liberal." But, we still know what a churl is. Our grandparents did, anyway. The New American Standard translation says "rogue." The New English Bible says "villain." The New English Bible's translation:

> The scoundrel will no longer be thought noble, nor the villain called a prince.

You get the idea. The Powers That Be in Isaiah's day were calling black white. After the Babylonians carted them off to Babylon about a century and a half later, they had seven decades to re-think their definitions. When you are forcibly moved from being the Powers That Be to Powers That Were, you have considerable time and motivation to re-think your first principles.

What we see here is the effect of Gramsci's strategy. The outside intellectuals who have set the standards of excellence for the world of Hollywood, not to mention television and the universities, have had enormous impact in Hollywood. The most powerful entertainment medium is being used to send a message. Because our generation of moguls and performers is far more self-conscious about its message, it has abandoned Samuel Goldwyn recommendation: "If you want to send a message, go see Western Union." Western Union has pretty much disappeared, and so has the old Hollywood.

Hollywood has been on the wrong side of the culture war twice: from 1920 to 1934, and from 1960 to the present. It cannot win this war. But it can lose its audience.

Conclusion

Antonio Gramsci had an agenda: furthering Communist revolution. His strategy was to undermine the West's confidence in its own institutions. He recognized that mass culture supports bourgeois civilization. It had to be undermined. He wanted to replace bourgeois civilization with Marxist civilization.

Gramsci's strategy of subversion has been implemented by Hollywood. I am not saying that studio heads have ever sat down and read a book by Gramsci. The only connection that a typical Hollywood mogul might have with Marx would be a video of *A Night at the Opera*. Nevertheless, Gramsci's strategy of cultural subversion has been implemented by Hollywood. It has also been implemented by the TV networks and some of the cable channels. Anyone who doubts this statement needs to spend one evening watching sitcom re-runs on Nick at Night, followed by an evening of prime-time sitcoms. As for an evening of MTV, nobody should require that much evidence. Ten minutes should do just fine.

The difference between Gramsci and the producers who have baptized filth in the name of either art or entertainment is this: Gramsci wanted to replace something he regarded as bad—bourgeois morality—with something better. Degradation was merely a weapon. Hollywood wants to replace bourgeois morality with degradation. But, for Hollywood, degradation is not a means to an end. It is the end, as in the goal. Christians see this and say, "if this continues, it really will be the end," as in the road.

After "The End" come the credits. Someday, God is going to roll the credits listing the names of all of the creative people who produced Hollywood's Gramscian extravaganza. This will be part of an awards show, which will have the highest audience rating in history: 100%. You can read about it in Revelation 20:11–15. I hope your name will not be in those credits. You should, too.

Notes

1. Karl Marx, "Reflections of a Young Man on the Choice of a Profession" (1835), in Karl Marx and Frederick Engels, *Collected Works* (New York: International Publishers, 1975), I, p. 3.

2. I discuss this in my book, *Marx's Religion of Revolution: Regeneration Through Chaos* (Tyler, Texas: Institute for Christian Economics, [1968] 1989), Appendix C: "The Myth of Marx's Poverty." Available free on www.freebooks.com.

3. Karl Marx, *Capital: A Critique of Political Economy* (Chicago: Charles H. Kerr, 1909), III, p. 1031.

4. Antonio Gramsci, "Marinetti the Revolutionary" (1921), in *Selections from Cultural Writings*, edited by David Forgacs and Geoffrey Nowell-Smith (Cambridge, Massachusetts: Harvard University Press, 1985), pp. 50–51.

5. Malachi Martin, *The Keys of This Blood* (New York: Simon & Schuster, 1990), ch. 13.

6. *Ibid.*, p. 245.

7. *Ibid.*, p. 250.

8. *Ibid.*, p. 251.

9. *Ibid.*, pp. 272–74.

10. Stéphane Courtois, et al., *The Black Book of Communism: Crimes, Terror, Repression* (Cambridge, Massachusetts: Harvard University Press, 1999).

11. Martin, *Keys of This Blood*, p. 259.

12. Augustine, *The City of God* (New York: Modern Library, 1950), II:4, p. 43.

13. Michael Medved, *Hollywood vs. America: Popular Culture and the War on Traditional Values* (New York: HarperCollins, 1992), pp. 21–22.

14. Gary North, *Is the World Running Down? Crisis in the Christian Worldview* (Tyler, Texas: Institute for Christian Economics, 1988). Available free on www. freebooks.com.

15. *Ibid.*, pp. 51–54.

16. *Ibid.*, pp. 56–58.

17. *Ibid.*, p. 58.

18. *Ibid.*, pp. 61–63.

19. *Ibid.*, p. 287.

20. *Ibid.*, p. 288.

21. *Ibid.*, p. 289.

22. *Ibid.*

23. *Ibid.*, p. 292.

24. Neal Gabler, *An Empire of Their Own: How the Jews Invented Hollywood* (New York: Crown, 1988), pp. 315–18.

The Neglected Market for Decency

Finally, brethren, whatsoever things are true, whatsoever things are honest, whatsoever things are just, whatsoever things are pure, whatsoever things are lovely, whatsoever things are of good report; if there be any virtue, and if there be any praise, think on these things (Philippians 4:8).

B Y THE COMMON grace of God, men agree on the basics of what constitutes righteousness, virtue, and the good life.[1] We know this because God told Moses that the Israelites would gain respect from the nations around them.

> Behold, I have taught you statutes and judgments, even as the LORD my God commanded me, that ye should do so in the land whither ye go to possess it. Keep therefore and do them; for this is your wisdom and your understanding in the sight of the nations, which shall hear all these statutes, and say, Surely this great nation is a wise and understanding people. For what nation is there so great, who hath God so nigh unto them, as the LORD our God is in all things that we call upon him for? And what nation is there so great, that hath statutes and

judgments so righteous as all this law, which I set before you this day? (Deuteronomy 4:5–8).[2]

This is why there will always be a market for decency. The question, then, is this: Will God-fearing people ever be in a position to sell to this market?

Freedom of Choice Without Much Choice

In the previous chapter, I cited at length the findings of Michael Medved regarding the consistently superior economic performance of PG-rated films. This information has not filtered down to the public, but it is inconceivable that it is not a well-known fact in Hollywood.

I have already provided my preliminary answer to the question: "Will Hollywood change?" I think this is unlikely. For over four decades, Hollywood has been engaged in on-screen guerilla warfare against the ideals and self-interest of ticket-buyers. Those buying the tickets have generally avoided such counter-measures as organized boycotts. The cost of organizing a boycott is high. The only visibly successful boycott was the one launched against *The Last Temptation of Christ*. But that movie was so appallingly awful that the free market probably would have killed it anyway.[3]

The traditional way for the would-be ticket-buyer to fight back is to stay home or attend a PG-rated film. Two by two, this is what customers have done. But the strategy has not worked. I offer these reasons. First, because the percentage of attendees has not varied for a generation. Nothing Hollywood has done has changed this. Any hope of changing this is now gone. So, it is cheaper institutionally to stick with the status quo.

Second, until *The Passion*, Christians have not had an explicitly Christian film to mobilize around. *Chariots of Fire* (1980) was Christian in its content, but the producers were not from Hollywood, and they went on to secular projects. They were not Christians self-consciously producing for a Christian market.

Third, the decision-makers in Hollywood are not Christians, nor are those people who provide them with their social status, however limited: movie reviewers, nationally known columnists, political leaders, academics, and artists. The social constraints on them lead them away from meeting economic demand from Christian ticket-buyers. They already have a lot of money personally. They are motivated by non-monetary sanctions, just so long as they don't lose money too often.

Fourth, the technology and skills relating to commercial film-making are possessed by a tiny number of people. While the monopoly enjoyed by the moguls of the golden age was far tighter than what their successors have today, the barriers to entry are still enormous. This keeps outsiders safely outside. Christians are outsiders.

Fifth, the sources of outside funding, mainly multinational banks, are controlled by people who are hostile to the Christian faith. The number of churches in New York City is small compared to the population. The number of Bible-believing Christian senior officers in multinational banks located in New York City is either minimal or nonexistent. This has been true for a century. It is not likely to change.

So, the existence of consumer demand has not been translated into supply. *The decision-makers are not motivated primarily by money.* This is true of most people most of the time. People prefer stability. They prefer familiar routines. They do not want to make major changes. They will make them, sometimes, if the alternative is bankruptcy or being fired. Even here, most people resist change and return to their old habits as soon as they can. "But it is happened unto them according to the true proverb, The dog is turned to his own vomit again; and the sow that was washed to her wallowing in the mire" (II Peter 2:22).

Yet there is still hope. *The Passion* has provided visible evidence that confirms this hope. As technology lowers the cost of all operations, as creative outsiders learn the necessary skills, as distribution becomes more direct through the World Wide Web, as financing becomes available from literally hundreds of thousands of Christians who now have a net worth of over five million dollars, and as the public realizes that ticket-money talks, the possibility of an alternative becomes more believable.

There is something else. In every field of endeavor, there is a very limited supply of top performers. No group has a natural monopoly over the supply of such people. Creative genius is randomly distributed, as far as human measurement is concerned. The United States remains the most entrepreneurial society on earth. This is its greatest strength, economically speaking. If the market for moral films and even explicitly Christian films really does exist, then entrepreneurs within the Christian community will be able to meet the demand of these presently thwarted ticket-buyers when the costs of entry get even lower. *Technology is on the side of decentralization, all over the world.* This will make it ever-more difficult for any insider group to maintain control over resources, especially that most valuable economic resource, human creativity.

Two generations ago, the world's first movie superstar wrote an article on the impossibility of the Hollywood Establishment to thwart the demand of ticket-buyers indefinitely. It is worth looking at that article today, seventy years after it was written. It seems almost prophetic in today's entertainment world, which is the post-*Passion* world. One week before *The Passion* was released, what you are about to read would have seemed far less plausible.

Mary Pickford's Predictions in 1934

Mary Pickford was the original movie superstar. She was a Canada-born actress who was known as America's sweetheart. In 1919, she, her husband Douglas Fairbanks, and a few others created United Artists, a film production and distribution company. It was the only company in Hollywood run by gentiles. She knew the business better than almost any other screen performer except her husband and Charlie Chaplain.

In 1934, the year that the so-called Hays Code governing on-screen morality began to be self-enforced by Hollywood's film industry, she wrote an article on the movies as both an art form and an industry. The article revealed her as a very bright, very principled, quite remarkable forecaster. She foresaw that television would not replace the movies, and would be a blessing to performers.

She had wise words to say about the arrival of industry self-censorship—self-censorship which was encouraged by the official threat of organized boycotts of offending movies by America's churches, both Protestant and Catholic. (As we have seen, the threat was a threat because it was rarely tested. The enforcers had more bark than bite.) She was convinced that good pictures had made money during the worst years of the Great Depression, 1931–33. She was also convinced that the threat of a boycott would reduce the supply of rotten pictures.

> Every picture of merit made since the depression engulfed us has met with financial success in spite of trying economic conditions and drastic criticism aimed at the industry from many quarters.
>
> Much of this criticism of course was warranted. In fact constructive criticism is a marvelous tonic. It is medicine, often bitter, and usually a pill that we hate to swallow. Still, had it not been for the church drive for decency, it is difficult to predict how drastic our disaster might have been. We had become so addicted to questionable wisecracks, so proud of insidious lines with double meanings, so lopsided with sophistication, and so befuddled by the vulgar viewpoint of that miasmic minority known as the "intelligentsia" that we completely lost sight of the fact that the majority audience of America is decent-minded.

She then made another prediction.

> Dirt and filth under the guise of humor will never be tolerated by a nation as young as ours. We are too naive nationally, still too wholesome in our point of view, to be swayed by that Continental cynicism which the sophisticate points to as the ne plus ultra of humor.

She may have been correct, but if she was, then this young nation grew up very fast. She died in 1979, long after the debauchery she did not think Americans would pay for had proven her wrong. But not completely wrong.

She was convinced that America's moral core is basically decent. She had faith in the taste of the American people. What they wanted then, she said, is a good story, told creatively on the silver screen.

Quite evidently we are still a Cinderella-minded nation. We love the triumph of virtue, the supremacy of success, especially when achieved at the end of an obstacle race. We are still childlike enough and healthy enough to enjoy laughter. The stonemasons of our industry are the producers, the directors, the writers, the stars. The keystone of the arch upon which they toil, however, is the story. And no arch will ever be stronger than the keystone which supports it. A faulty story will cause the collapse of any arch, the downfall of the most adroit mason.[4]

Today, we are still putting her confidence in us to the test. My book is about this time of testing. It is not clear yet whether she was correct, or whether the most eloquent cynic of her generation, H. L. Mencken, was correct: "No one in this world, so far as I know—and I have researched the records for years, and employed agents to help me—has ever lost money by underestimating the intelligence of the great masses of the plain people." Mencken was a follower of the philologist-turned-philosopher, Friedrich Nietzsche, who made famous the phrase, "God is dead."

After the Good Old Days

The first decade of the Hays Code is known as the golden age of Hollywood. Some film historians might extend this assessment into the late 1940s. When television began eating into the industry's audience and profits, the golden age turned silver. Using the classification of the image of Nebuchadnezzar dream (Daniel 2) as a guide, I would say that by 1965, Hollywood was well into its bronze stage. By 1980, iron. Today? Iron mixed with clay. Nevertheless, here and there, gold nuggets have been mined from this visibly depleted mine.

Let us not wax too nostalgic about Hollywood's golden age. The best of the movies were great. *Casablanca* is one of the great ones. It is overwhelmingly the film most quoted by today's writers. This should not come as a shock, any more than Claude Rains should have been shocked by the gambling in the back room at Rick's. Most of the movies from that era that we still watch were good: *Gone With the Wind, The Wizard of Oz, Gunga Din*, to name three of the bonanza year of 1939. But when I say "great," I have in mind positive movies that shaped people's perception of the way the world ought to be, but which also were artistically good enough to become classics. Here, there are not many that we still rent and watch. I doubt that any of them had the impact of *Ben-Hur* (1959), either artistically or at the box office. From a strictly Christian point of view, one film stands out above all the rest: *A Man Called Peter* (1955), based on Catherine Marshall's biography of her husband, who served as Chaplain of the U.S. Senate, 1947–49. There have never been on-screen sermon extracts to match that film. But it is not regarded as a classic.

There have been better movies than the pre-1960 ones from the point of view of both artistry and message. The one that stands out above the rest is *Chariots of Fire* (1980), a British-made film that had not one famous star. It came out of nowhere to win the Oscar as Best Picture in 1981. It truly blindsided Hollywood. It was loosely based on two careers in track: Eric Liddell of Scotland and Harold Abrahams of England. Each man won a gold medal at the 1924 Olympics. Liddell later went on to be a Congregationalist missionary in China, where he died in a Japanese prison camp in 1945. In one of those strange casting decisions, a Catholic played the Jew, and a homosexual played the Christian. But the public did not know this, and still doesn't. The movie centers around Liddell's decision not to run in his top-rated event, the 100-meter dash, because the preliminary heats were held on a Sunday. The story was true, but the movie's version is not: a last-minute switch. In fact, Liddell had trained for months to qualify in the 400-meter race.

This movie was marketed shrewdly. The distributor invited the nation's pastors to attend a special local afternoon showing. I attended one of these invitational showings as a layman. In city after city, pastors who attended were asked to tell their congregations about the film. Churches were offered discounts for bulk ticket purchases. The strategy worked. The film made a great deal of money with relatively little advertising. The biggest mistake that the distributor made was to revoke the policy of low-cost purchases through churches after the film won the Oscar. Attendance dropped off rapidly after this.

Hollywood saw all this and yawned. "It was a fluke," the experts said.

The next breakthrough was *Tender Mercies* (1983). Robert Duvall won the Oscar for Best Actor in 1984 for his portrayal of a country music writer who hit rock bottom in a small West Texas community. Because of his sense of moral obligation to work off his debts, he stopped drinking, went to church, got baptized, married the widow who had helped him straighten out, and started writing songs again. There was tragedy in the film, but there was also redemption. Horton Foote won an Oscar for best screenplay.

Foote is a master, with a career beginning in the late 1930s and extending, for all I know, to next week. He still lives in the little wood frame house in Texas that he grew up in. He wrote the screenplay for the film that Duvall regards as his best film, the incredibly low budget *Tomorrow* (1972), an adaptation of William Faulkner's 1939 story. He wrote the screenplay for Harper Lee's novel, *To Kill a Mockingbird*, the 1962 movie that won Gregory Peck an Oscar. So did Foote. The movie is usually in any top 20 American films list. He wrote the screenplay for *The Trip to Bountiful* (1985), which won Geraldine Page her Oscar for Best Actress.

His screenplays are stories about low-key real world people who might live next door if you happen to live in a small southern town. They face moral decisions, and they deal with them morally. If he is a Christian, he does not talk about it in his autobiography, *Beginnings* (2001), but that thin volume takes us only to 1943. There is no question that he understands and respects the Protestant Christianity of the small southern town.

Other mid-1980s movies that did not assault our sensibilities and also raised our spirits include *Gandhi* (1984), which earned Ben Kingsley an Oscar, and *The Natural* (1984), with Robert Redford playing an aging but spectacular baseball player who makes a comeback from a career that had been sidetracked before it ever really began. It is a story of good vs. evil, light vs. darkness. In the movie, good triumphs. These were highly successful movies at the box office.

Stephen Spielberg's movies are usually successful financially and rarely assault or insult the viewers. *Saving Private Ryan* surely brings to life D-Day and its immediate aftermath. It is a testament for my father's generation. I took my father to see it. He tends to doze off. I told him, "You won't doze off in the first 20 minutes of this movie." He didn't, or anytime later. There is no question that the language was accurate, which means filled with Army expletives, including FUBAR. Yet this language was not an assault on our ears, precisely because it was an historical re-creation. The language was consistent with the events taking place on-screen. They did not seem out of place. A case can be made that this language could have been avoided, and on the whole, I think it should have been. It was not absolutely necessary to the success of the movie. But, then again, could *Patton* have come close to the man, had the Hays Code been enforced? His language was legendary. The script writers actually toned down his opening speech in front of the huge American flag. The original speech was much worse. My point is this: there is a difference between the use of obscenities as part of a believable historical re-creation vs. what we heard in the gangster movie, *Goodfellas*. There is a difference between a movie with foul language and a movie that makes the viewers feel foul. The public understands this difference. But does Hollywood? Not often enough. When it comes to Hollywood, it's consistently FUBAR, or at least SNAFU.

Then we come to *The Lord of the Rings*. A Catholic professor of medieval literature wrote it. Before submitting it for publication, he read it to a group of intimate friends that included another professor of medieval literature, C. S. Lewis. The trilogy gained a huge audience a decade after he published it in 1954. The readership has continued to grow. Books related to the series are now part of a cottage industry. The movie's director had gained his skills by making low-budget horror movies that were seen by very few. The series has no nudity, no foul language, but considerable violence, none of it gratuitous. For three years in a row, the films have gained huge revenues, wide acclaim, and little criticism, not even for their violence. The series is a true phenomenon, like nothing else in movie history. The combination of visual artistry, good acting, amazing special effects, spectacular scenery, and a solid plot has made it the standard of the industry and perhaps even the medium of film. About the only person I have ever heard of who did not particularly like the films is me. (Many years ago, I bought a copy of Lampoon's *Bored of the Rings*. I could not get up enough interest to read it. But my teenage son did, who also read the entire series repeatedly.)

These movies are representative of what Hollywood can do, excepting only *Gandhi*, which was not Hollywood-produced. When a combination of factors leads to the production of films like these, producers make fortunes and viewers get more than their money's worth. It does not take a Hollywood-type budget to make a Horton Foote movie. It just takes the willingness to stick to his text. His text does not violate the Hays Code, at least not in a way that anyone notices.

This information is a prelude to the topic at hand: how Mel Gibson has identified the existence of an enormous market for high quality Christian films, and how to tap into it without going to or through Hollywood.

High Artistry on a Low Budget

Mel Gibson, as an independent producer of far greater financial means today than he possessed on the day before the release of *The Passion*, has unquestionably proven this contention by Miss Pickford:

> Perhaps the greatest thing about motion pictures is that no one can ever have a monopoly on ideas. Masterpieces cannot be made to order. Artistic supremacy hovers for a season over one studio, then producers bang away with their inspirational guns and chase it to another, where it perches precariously, a harried quarry soon to wing its way elsewhere, ceaselessly pursued by these diligent huntsmen.[5]

Gibson has proven himself to be a diligent huntsman. He produced a movie that looks like a $100 million budget film, yet he did this for under $30 million. He will reap a huge gain on his investment. He made the movie without a "bankable" star. He is so good at directing that he produced a blockbuster on a mini-budget.

Had he not been confident in the truth of his film's message, he would not have produced it. Had he not been immune to the lure of money—measured by the fear of losing it—he would not have produced it. It was because he was willing to lose all that money in a religious cause that he produced a bonanza for himself, both artistically and financially. In this sense, he applied Christ's formula for success:

> Then said Jesus unto his disciples, If any man will come after me, let him deny himself, and take up his cross, and follow me. For whosoever will save his life shall lose it: and whosoever will lose his life for my sake shall find it (Matthew 16:24–25).

This was a command based on the promise of a positive sanction: life. Gibson took up his cross: investing $30 million to present the story of another man who took up a cross.

Jesus' command was followed by the promise of a negative sanction:

> For what is a man profited, if he shall gain the whole world, and lose his own soul? or what shall a man give in exchange for his soul (Matthew 16:26)?

The box office success of *The Passion* has dumbfounded Hollywood. What had looked like a sure loser to the movie-production experts turned out to be a blockbuster. They completely missed the boat. They did not see what would happen. How did this happen? Because of a combination of factors:

> The subject matter: a perennial theme
> A faithfully confrontational telling of the story
> A potentially large audience: Christians
> Gibson's skill as a director
> The skills of the crew
> The publicity his critics generated: "buzz"

The willingness of theaters to screen it

The curiosity of the general public

Post-screening word of mouth: "buzz"

The timing of the release: low competition

His decision to provide subtitles

So completely did Hollywood miss this boat that the ship they are on looks like the ship of fools. They initially ignored the movie. Then they ridiculed the movie. Then they slandered the movie. Then they saw it make $117 million in five days—the weekend of the Oscars. Hollywood handed out eleven Oscars to a New Zealand director's product, based on an English Catholic's novel, and wondered: "How can we pretend that *The Passion* was never made when Oscar time comes next year?"

The Christian community has seen that the film is better than what the critics had said. They read the subtitles, and they recognize most of the words of Jesus. These are the words we find in the gospels. So, more than any previous Hollywood version of the crucifixion, this one is closest to the text.

Some Christians have not been surprised. They knew that most of the film's critics are liberals, both theologically and politically. These critics have no understanding of the basic tenets of Christianity. They do not understand the on-screen words that begin the movie.

> But he was wounded for our transgressions, he was bruised for our iniquities: the chastisement of our peace was upon him; and with his stripes we are healed (Isaiah 53:5).

They do not attend church. They do not pray. They surely do not tithe. They are no more reliable as witnesses to the movie than the false witnesses in the Jewish court were in the movie. They are not to be trusted.

The magnitude of the discrepancy between what the critics wrote and what the viewer sees is enormous. The viewer trusted Mel Gibson to deliver the goods. Gibson did. Now, in retrospect, the negative reviewers appear as people belonging to a confederation of dunces. Their hatred of the film's message—a message to which hundreds of millions of Christians, worldwide, have committed themselves—made them unreliable judges. That which conservative Christians have known for years is now a matter of public record. The whole world now knows. *The Passion* was subject to a media lynching by the Establishment media. The trouble is, their rope was made of silly putty.

Undermining the System of Control

The humanists who for decades had censored in advance any information that they found inconvenient got blown out of the water by the Internet. There was a symbol of this unexpected transformation: Matt Drudge. When Drudge unspiked the *Newsweek* article that had named Monica Lewinsky as President Clinton's sexual victim, he sent the Establishment news media a message: "Your days of wine and roses are numbered." The ability of the news media to suppress a story has now been dramatically reduced by the low cost of putting up a Web site and clicking the Forward button. The cost of suppression has gone up beyond the ability of the gatekeepers to guard the gates. This has created a nightmare for the news industry. The Web has cut into their ability to sell newspapers and generate an audience for the evening news. The Establishment news industry is hemorrhaging. The Web is siphoning off paying subscribers. It is also reducing the number of unquestioning believers.

This has begun to change the nature of rulership. The established chains of command depend on self-government by those under authority. The public is expected to obey the law, believe whatever it is told by those in charge, and pay taxes to support the existing Establishment. But there are rumblings out there from people who are beginning to opt out from under control by the established hierarchies.

The movie industry and television are the most pervasive cultural media in our day. They offer both images and sound. They are readily believed. How can images and sound lie? But, of course, they can lie. Those who create the images and the sound create virtual reality. Virtual reality can readily become real propaganda.

Our opponents understand how powerful screen images are. This is why they did whatever they could to get Gibson to re-write his script, and after this failed (in most cases), to pillory Gibson for sticking with the New Testament text. It is not Gibson's "artistic license" with the New Testament texts that has called forth most of the criticism. On the contrary, it is his faithfulness to those texts that has outraged the critics.

Conclusion

Mel Gibson is not part of Hollywood, either geographically or confessionally. He does not answer to Hollywood, nor does he search for recognition in Hollywood, let alone the dark corners of secular humanism in which today's moguls seek others' affirmation. He had heard the long-ignored message that had been sent by the public. He had saved lots of the money that enthusiastic viewers had sent him, by way of Hollywood. Then he put his money where his heart was.

The artistic question now is this: "Will Hollywood's media elite follow his lead?" I have my doubts. But I also am confident that Miss Pickford's assessment of the power of the free market will win out in the end. Hollywood may choose to thumb its collective nose at ticket-buyers who do not share Hollywood's view of the world, but the nose-thumbers will not do so at zero price. *Hollywood had better give us what we want if it wants to make money.* But what do most viewers want? Miss Pickford called it right. "The world wants simple, human screen fare, fundamental in emotion and wholesome in motivation. But the world does not want—and will not accept—a standard pattern."

The Passion of the Christ is surely not the standard pattern. This is why the critics are outraged. Gibson stuck too closely to the texts of the New Testament. He produced a visually compelling film that uses subtitles, which people are compelled to read in order to follow the story. These subtitles include the words that all previous Hollywood versions of the crucifixion neglected to put into the script. This, above all, is Hollywood's complaint against *The Passion*.

If there is one scene in *The Passion* that represents Hollywood's attitude toward the movie and all that it represents, it is the scene where Pilate offers to release one prisoner: Jesus or the murderer Barabbas. The crowd is unanimous: "Give us Barabbas!" Hollywood has been shouting this since 1960.

Tens of millions of us are really very tired of Barabbas. Our numbers are growing.

Notes

1. Gary North, *Dominion and Common Grace: The Biblical Basis of Progress* (Tyler, Texas: Institute for Christian Economics, 1987). This is available free at www.freebooks.com.

2. Gary North, *Inheritance and Dominion: An Economic Commentary on Deuteronomy* (Harrisonburg, Virginia: Dominion Educational Ministries, Inc., 2003), ch. 8. Available for free at www.demischools.org/deuteronomy-v1.pdf.

3. See Chapter 8.

4. Mary Pickford, "The Big Bad Wolf Has Been Muzzled" (1934), on *Hollywood Renegades Archive*. http://tinyurl.com/yumlw

5. Mary Pickford, "The Big Bad Wolf Has Been Muzzled" (1934), on *Hollywood Renegades Archive*. http://tinyurl.com/yumlw

Part 3

A Christian Counter-Attack

8

Two Christs, Two Boycotts

Then if any man shall say unto you, Lo, here is Christ, or there; believe it not. For there shall arise false Christs, and false prophets, and shall shew great signs and wonders; insomuch that, if it were possible, they shall deceive the very elect. Behold, I have told you before. Wherefore if they shall say unto you, Behold, he is in the desert; go not forth: behold, he is in the secret chambers; believe it not (Matthew 24:23–26).

THE CONTEXT OF Jesus' teaching here was the messianism of His day. The land of Israel had its share of would-be messiahs and social redeemers, a fact mentioned by Gamaliel to the Sanhedrin (Acts 5:36–37). Jesus warned His followers not to be deceived by these people. There is only one Messiah. Who is this Messiah? Jesus gave the correct answer shortly thereafter.

But he held his peace, and answered nothing. Again the high priest asked him, and said unto him, Art thou the Christ, the Son of the Blessed? And Jesus said, I am: and ye shall see the Son of man sitting on the right hand of power, and coming in the clouds of heaven (Mark 14:61–62).

The lure of false messiahs is great. Modern America is afflicted with them still. Jim Jones was one. Almost a thousand of his followers died in one of the most remarkable events of the twentieth century: mass suicide.

There is another way for false messiahs to gain followers. That is for those who offer secular redemption to confuse people by means of a false view of the true Messiah. If you can persuade men to reject the true Messiah by retroactively turning Him into a anxiety-filled modern man—possibly with sandals, although without leather patches on the elbows of his tweed sports jacket—then one of your spiritual colleagues can later offer them redemption through politics or psychology or some other hoped-for method that promises to change the nature of man by manipulating his environment.

With this in mind, let us turn to the story of *The Last Temptation of Christ*.

First, the Book

The author of the book, Nikos Kazantzakis, was a spiritual rebel against the Greek Orthodox Church. He was converted to Darwinism as a student, then to the philosophy of Nietzsche, then to Communism, but always with a mixture of atheism and sexual libertinism.[1] In 1945, he served as the General Minister of Education for Greece. He died in 1957.

He gained worldwide fame posthumously, when the 1964 movie version of his novel, *Zorba the Greek*, won seven Oscar nominations in 1965, including best picture, and won three of them, including best supporting actress. The movie is not often shown on TV, and I do not recall seeing it in a video rental store. Then again, I have never looked for it. It was a depressing tale about Zorba, a big-talking failure in Greece, who lures a hapless British investor into a disastrous economic scheme. There is also a sub-plot about the outsider's love for a local woman, who has her throat slashed by a jealous rival after church. The rival is not brought to justice. Whenever Zorba is sad or confused, he dances. His victim ends the movie by finally dancing alone. Anthony Quinn and Alan Bates gave fine performances, but despite my appreciation for Bates as an actor, I decided that I would never watch that depressing movie again. I never have. It remains a good example of Hollywood's pretensions at art in the brief era when the Hays Production Code was unofficially being scrapped. In 1966, the Code was officially abandoned. The movie was hailed by reviewers, and still is, as an affirmation of Zorba's love of life. My assessment is different:

> But he that sinneth against me wrongeth his own soul: all they that hate me love death (Proverbs 8:36).

The Last Temptation of Christ (1950) was translated into English in 1960. I regard it as the most blasphemous book ever published by a mainstream publisher in the name of art. Fortunately, from the point of view of Christians, it is so poorly written that to describe it as both tedious and turgid would give it too much credit. It is a 500-page excursion into the mind of an author who hated God even more than he hated a coherent story line.

Here is the basic theme. Jesus, the son of Mary, is a carpenter who makes his living selling crosses to the Romans for crucifying Jews. He is a confused young man. His friend and counsellor, Judas, keeps telling him to stop making crosses for a living.[2] But Jesus is a deeply frustrated man. He fell in love with Mary Magdalene, a prostitute daughter of a rabbi, who became a prostitute because she was so sexually aroused by Jesus when she was age four and he was age three that she could not stay away from men. She and Jesus had touched the soles of their feet together, and this was all it took to corrupt poor Mary. He confesses to her father, a rabbi,

> It must have been when I was three years old. I slipped into your house at a time when no one was home. I took Magdalene by the hand; we undressed and lay down on the ground, pressing together the soles of our naked feet. What joy that was, what a joyful sin! From that time on Magdalene was lost; she was lost—she could no longer live without a man, without men.[3]

Jesus therefore feels very guilty. The author implicitly asks, "Can we blame him?"

So far, you might regard the book as the product of a deranged pedophilic foot-fetishist. You would be wrong. The author was far more self-conscious in his rebellion against God than a mere sexual deviant is. Let us continue.

Jesus then confesses to the rabbi, that he had at one time prayed to God,

> God, make me God! God, make me God! God, make me God![4]

Therefore, he declares,

> I am lucifer. Me! Me![5]

The book is the story of how Jesus, through a series of rebellions, achieves his goal of becoming God. He achieves it at his last temptation on the cross. When on the cross he sees Peter tell Judas—you remember Judas, don't you?—"Let's go. Judas, step in front, lead us!"[6] Jesus, hanging on the cross, is then released by a guardian angel. Then he is allowed to live a normal life. He almost married Mary Magdalene, except that the would-be Apostle Paul, still stuck in his role as Saul, had put together a mob that stoned her to death.[7] But that turned out all right after all, because the angel then revealed to Jesus the following truth about women, which he had somehow missed:

> "Be patient," he said, "submit, do not despair. Only one woman exists in the world, one woman with countless faces. This one falls; the next rises. Mary Magdalene died, Mary sister of Lazarus lives and waits for us, waits for you. She is Magdalene herself, but with another face. Listen . . . let us go and comfort her. Within her womb she holds—holds for you, Jesus of Nazareth—the greatest of all joys: a son—your son, Let us go!"[8]

So, you lose some but win some. The lesson is clear. You've got to know when to hold 'em, know when to fold 'em, know when to walk away, know when to run. Jesus ran in chapters 30 through 33. But then he stopped running. He decided to take his medicine. He got nailed to the cross again. His aged disciples came out to shout at him: "Coward, deserter, traitor!"

No, wait. Jesus never got off the cross at all. He never got old. It was all a dream sent by the devil.

> Temptation had captured him for a split second [actually, four boring chapters—G.N.] and led him astray. The joys, marriages and children were lies; the decrepit, degraded old men who shouted coward, deserter, traitor at him were all lies. All—all were illusions sent by the Devil. His disciples were alive and thriving. They had gone over sea and land and were proclaiming the Good News. Everything had turned out as it should, glory be to God!
>
> He uttered a triumphant cry: IT IS ACCOMPLISHED!
>
> And it was as though he had said: Everything had begun.[9]

THE END

All right, I made up some of this. I made up THE END. The book merely ends.

An extended dream sequence just before death: how semi-creative! It had worked so well for Ambrose Bierce in "An Occurrence at Owl Creek Bridge" in the late nineteenth century that Kazantzakis decided to use it again.

Here is Kazantzakis' Jesus' self-testimony.

> The kingdom of heaven? . . . I don't care about the kingdom of heaven. I like the earth. I want to marry, I tell you; I want Magdalene, even if she's a prostitute. It's my fault she became one, my fault, and I shall save her. Her! Not the earth, not the kingdom of this world—It's Magdalene I want to save. That's enough for me![10]

I must save you, Magdalene—oh, if I could only do it!—you, Magdalene, not the race of Israel: that I cannot save. I'm no prophet. If I open my mouth, I have no idea what to say. God did not anoint my lips with burning coals, did not cast his thunderbolt into my bowels to make me burn, rush frenzied into the streets and begin to shout.[11]

I'm a liar, a hypocrite, I'm afraid of my own shadow, I never tell the truth—I don't have the courage. When I see a woman go by, I blush and lower my head, but my eyes fill with lust. I never lift my hand to plunder or to thrash or kill—not because I don't want to but because I'm afraid. I want to rebel against my mother, the centurion, God—but I'm afraid. Afraid! Afraid! If you look inside me, you'll see Fear, a trembling rabbit, sitting in my bowels—Fear, nothing else. That is my father, my mother and my God.[12]

I, too, was once a woman, in another life, and I used to weave.[13]

The Jesus of Kazantzakis declares a comforting doctrine: there is no final judgment. Above all, there is no hell. Jesus in the Gospel of Luke preached the doctrine of hell in the parable of the poor man, Lazarus, and the unnamed rich man. Kazantzakis takes this parable, found in Luke 16, and reverses it. In the original parable, the rich man is in hell, and he cries out to Lazarus to put a drop of water on his tongue. Abraham tells him that this is impossible. A fixed gulf exists forever between heaven and hell. This is the longest passage in the New Testament on hell. This teaching was unique. Jesus was its originator. Kazantzakis' Jesus presents another ending. Lazarus calls on God to refresh the condemned man.

'God, how can anyone be happy in Paradise when he knows that there is a man—a soul—roasting for all eternity? Refresh him, Lord, that I may be refreshed. Deliver him, Lord, that I may be delivered. Otherwise I too shall begin to feel the flames.' God heard his thought and was glad. 'Lazarus, beloved,' he said, 'go down; take the thirster by the hand. My fountains are inexhaustible. Bring him here so that he may drink and refresh himself, and you refresh yourself with him' . . . 'For all eternity?' asked Lazarus. 'Yes, for all eternity,' God replied.[14]

So, nobody can be happy in heaven if there is even one person in hell. Therefore, in order to redeem all those in heaven, God will redeem all those in hell. This is the gospel—good news—according to St. Nikos.

A parallel re-write is his version of Christ's parable of the ten virgins with lamps. They await the return of the Bridegroom. Five had filled their lamps with oil. Five had not. The Bridegroom then returns. The virgins with no oil ask those who had oil to share their oil. They refuse. The five foolish virgins then run to town to get oil. They come back too late: the wedding has already begun.

> Afterward came also the other virgins, saying, Lord, Lord, open to us. But he answered and said, Verily I say unto you, I know you not. Watch therefore, for ye know neither the day nor the hour wherein the Son of man cometh (Matthew 25:11–13).

This was not the way Kazantzakis wanted to hear it, so he re-wrote it. He has Jesus ask Nathaniel what he would have done to the foolish virgins. "I would have opened the door." Jesus replies: "Congratulations, friend Nathaniel."[15] But letting them in was not enough. They had to be honored. They "were the only ones to have their tired feet washed by the servants."[16]

Kazantzakis was thoroughly modern Nikos. The doctrine, above all other Christian doctrines, that he despised was the doctrine of hell. He shared this opinion with all of the modern world of humanism.

To this theology of a cosmos without permanent negative sanctions, he added a bit of pantheism. His Jesus felt pity for animals. Judas pressed him. Did he feel pity for ants?

> "Yes, for the ants too. Everything is God's. When I bend over the ant, inside his black, shiny eye I see the face of God."[17]

If Kazantzakis really believed this, he would have spent more time stomping on ants.

The author also revived that most ancient of heresies: to be as God (Genesis 3:5). He called for man's union with God. This is the heresy of both gnosticism and Hinduism. He began his book with these words:

> The dual substance of Christ—the yearning, so human, so super-human, of man to attain God or, more exactly, to return to God and identify himself with him—has always been a deep inscrutable mystery to me. . . . Every man partakes of the divine nature in both his spirit and his flesh. That is why the mystery of Christ is not simply for a particular creed: it is universal.[18]

> Struggle between the flesh and the spirit, rebellion and resistance, reconciliation and submission, and finally—the supreme purpose of the struggle—union with God: this was the ascent taken by Christ, the ascent which he invites us to take as well, following in his bloody tracks.[19]

This is an updated version of the ancient heresy of Nestorianism, which was condemned at the Council of Ephesis in 431 A.D. Nestorius denied the incarnation of God the Word. He placed the two natures of Christ—man and God—alongside each other. There was no true union. God was in some way united to man, but He was not *made* man, contrary to the doctrine of the incarnation. But if union was not inherent with Christ, then Jesus as a man somehow succeeded in uniting himself with God in history. This is Kazantzakis' theology, except that he acknowledged men as sinful, something that Nestorius did not affirm of Christ's humanity. Fallen man, by his own works, can become God. There is no heresy worse than this one. Kazantzakis affirmed it openly. "This is the Supreme Duty of the man who struggles—to set out for the lofty peak which Christ, the first-born son of salvation, attained."[20]

In raising fallen man to divinity, he pulled God down into fallen humanity. His Jesus announces,

Father and son are of the same root. Together they rise to heaven, together they descend to hell. If you strike one, both are wounded; if one makes a mistake, both are punished.[21]

Second, the Movie

When the Christian community learned in 1988 that Hollywood planned to release a film version of *The Last Temptation of Christ*, there was immediate opposition. Michael Medved devotes Chapter 3 of his book, *Hollywood vs. America*, to a detailed discussion of the events surrounding this protest. Chapter 3 begins the section of his book titled "The Attack on Religion." The chapter is titled, "A Declaration of War." He correctly sees this declaration as having come from Hollywood.

On August 11, 1988, there was an organized protest of 25,000 people at Universal City. This was the largest protest crowd ever assembled against a movie. Medved says that a friend of his who worked at Universal said the staff was apprehensive, expecting violence. There was none. The protesters sang hymns, listened to speeches, and went home. Medved comments:

> The media moguls, together with many of their supporters in the news media, persisted in dismissing the demonstrators (and all others opposed to the production and release of *The Last Temptation of Christ*) as representatives of a lunatic fringe of religious fanatics and right-wing extremists. In one typical piece of commentary, columnist Mike Duffy of the *Detroit Free Press* decried those who criticized the film as "sour, fun-loathing people" and "the American ignoramus faction that is perpetually geeked up on self-righteous bile. . . .
>
> "They looked for Reds under every bed with Joe McCarthy.
>
> "They cheered police dogs in Selma."
>
> "And now the know-nothing wacky pack has latched onto Martin Scorsese and *The Last Temptation of Christ*.[22]

One church petitioned the studio not to release the film. It collected 135,000 signatures. The studio ignored this petition.[23] Jack Valenti issued this statement:

> The key issue, the only issue, is whether or not self-appointed groups can prevent a film from being exhibited to the public. . . . The major companies of the MPAA support MCA/Universal in its absolute right to offer the people whatever movie it chooses.[24]

Mr. Valenti forgot another key issue: the absolute right of self-appointed groups to organize a national boycott.

Let me give a personal account. In the East Texas city where I lived in 1988, local fundamentalist churches organized a boycott. They informed the managers of every theater that if they showed this movie, the petitioners guaranteed that they would not attend that theater for a year. I did not see a copy of the letter, but a local minister informed a group of us about it. One manager ignored the petition. I did not attend that theater for one year. The theater closed within two years. It never got back all of its customers. The building was turned into a retail mini-mall.

Universal Pictures had a Constitutional right to release that movie, according to the Supreme Court—I mean the one in Washington. The public also had a legal right not to pay money to see it. Medved estimates that the movie lost a minimum of $10 million.[25]

He also relates his personal experience in reviewing the movie. He and a dozen other movie critics were invited to view the movie two weeks before its release. The lights dimmed. The movie began. The initial scene was of Christ, the cross-maker. He carries the top bar to a crucifixion. He stands beneath the dying man. He gets covered with blood. The movie lasted almost three hours. It was marked, Medved says, by "appalling boredom, laughable dialogue, and unbearably bad acting."

I finally broke down and rented the movie, which I saw today, in preparation for writing this chapter. (Movie reviewers should see the movies they review, I always say.) I can add only this: most of the dialogue is taken straight out of the novel. The screenwriter, Paul Schrader, a lapsed Dutch-American Calvinist, remained remarkably faithful to the novel. (He also wrote the screenplays for Scorsese's *Taxi Driver* and his most acclaimed film, *Raging Bull*. His Michigan Calvinist background is the setting for his 1979 movie, *Hardcore*, starring George C. Scott.)

Medved lists a series of preposterous scenes, such as the one where Jesus reaches into his tunic and pulls out his own heart.

> In response to such memorably miscalculated movie moments, some of my generally restrained colleagues, who attended the same critics' screening I did, began snickering, hooting, and laughing aloud midway through the picture's all-but-insufferable length.[26]

But, much to his amazement, when many of these same critics wrote their reviews, they gave the film a big send-up. One of them offered this explanation:

> Look, I know the picture's a dog. We both know that, and probably Scorsese knows it, too. But with all the Christian crazies shooting at him from every direction, I'm not going to knock him in public. If I slammed the picture too hard, then people would associate me with Falwell—and there's no way I'm ready for that.[27]

The Motion Picture Academy nominated Scorsese for the Oscar for Best Director. He did not win. Let me say, here and now, that Scorsese was cheated. He should have won. He did what every director should do. He remained remarkably faithful to the book. The book was tedious. So was the movie. The book's plot line was incoherent. So was the movie's. The book was filled with nutty theology, including God's face in an ant's eye. So was the movie. It was as if Scorsese had told Shrader, "Let's let the audience experience how slowly time passes when you're nailed to a cross. Make them suffer." Shrader performed magnificently. So did the actors. I can fault Scorsese on only one thing, aesthetically speaking: the movie looked like one of those low-budget Italian Hercules movies. I kept looking for Steve Reeves.

He did leave out some things. For instance, Kazantzakis is highly critical of the Judaism of Jesus' day. Consider his treatment of the Passover.

> The first day was all psalms, prayers and prostrations; and Jehovah, invisible, strode joyously into the tents and celebrated too, eating and drinking with his lips and wiping his beard. But starting with the second day and third days, the excessive meat and wine went to the heads of the people. The dirty jokes and the laughter and the bawdy tavern songs began, and men and women shamelessly and in broad daylight, at first within the tents, and then openly in the roads and on the green grass. In every neighborhood the celebrated prostitutes of Jerusalem appeared, plastered with make-up and smeared with aromatic oil.[28]

This ended up on the cutting room floor, assuming that it was ever filmed at all.

How to Wash One's Hand of All Responsibility

The book's publisher was careful to print this warning:

> This book is a work of fiction. Names, characters, places, and incidents either are products of the author's imagination or are used fictitiously. Any resemblance to actual events or locales or persons, living or dead, is entirely coincidental.

The movie followed suit. It ran the introductory words by Kazantzakis.

> The dual substance of Christ—the yearning, so human, so superhuman, of man to attain God or, more exactly, to return to God and identify himself with him—has always been a deep inscrutable mystery to me. . . .

Then it added:

> This film is not based upon the Gospels but upon the fictional explanation of the eternal spiritual conflict.

Consider another possible artistic effort. What if Mel Gibson had produced a film with this theme? Eva Braun, the daughter of the Chief Rabbi of Germany, seeks to serve her people as a reincarnated Esther. Initially, she tries to marry Adolph Hitler, in order to influence him, but then decides that Himmler has better economic prospects. She marries him instead. The rabbi, frantically trying to get his daughter back from such a brute, approaches Hitler and makes a deal. If Hitler will get the marriage annulled, the rabbi will arrange for Hitler to get low-cost slave labor from the synagogues. Hitler agrees. The marriage is annulled. The rabbi then writes Hitler's 1934 emergency laws. The freight trains roll.

Question: Would Gibson have gotten off the ethical hook merely by posting the disclaimers? Or would this defense have worked? "Look, this is a work of art, not history." Would Jack Valenti have issued this statement?

> The key issue, the only issue, is whether or not self-appointed groups can prevent a film from being exhibited to the public. . . . The major companies of the MPAA support Icon/Newmarket in their absolute right to offer the people whatever movie they choose.

Two Forms of Boycott

Hollywood knew that it could not prevent the distribution of *The Passion*. No company in Hollywood was willing to act as distributor. But it could do nothing about Newmarket Films, a New York company formed in the summer of 2002, from acting as the distributor. The anonymous studio heads had their response: never to work with Gibson again. Hollywood had to rely on media reviewers to discredit the film, preferably before it hit the theaters.

This has been the boycott strategy of every Establishment for five thousand years. Those with control over an industry can control what gets produced. If a group of people who think alike control the major media—newspapers, television networks, and film—they can nip undesirable ideas and images in the bud. No one cries "censorship," because the government is not involved, at least not directly. (The Federal Communication's Commission does license television networks' ownership of valuable airwaves, a monopoly for which the networks do not pay.) It is all done behind the scenes. The old boy network runs its boycotts from the top. They do not burn books, you understand. That would be much too crass. They just keep books from being published.

We should thank God for the Internet. The age-old strategy is coming to an end. No more ink. No more paper. No more distribution network. Dorothy and her friends are entering a dark forest. "Printers and toner and chips, oh my!"

Consumers must organize their boycotts from the bottom. This is difficult to do. Telling Americans what to do is always an iffy venture. I am not sure that the boycott against *The Last Temptation of Christ* was successful. It just looked successful. It was a stinkeroo of a movie based on an even worse stinkeroo of a book. I don't think a rave review from the Pope could have gotten that box office bomb into the black financially.

What works in favor of consumers is this: their taste prevents most morally evil movies from breaking even. For all their talent when they have morally sound scripts to work with, or even morally questionable scripts, Hollywood directors only rarely can translate self-conscious debauchery to the screen and still have a product that people will pay for. Word gets out, and it gets out fast—usually before the opening weekend is over. The Internet now gets word out even faster.

Mary Pickford had it right in 1934: morally sound movies make money. Morally debauched movies do not. She was not speaking of a mail order-distributed technology such as a videocassette or a DVD. She was not talking about materials that were once advertised as being sent in a plain brown wrapper. She was talking about the silver screen.

Conclusion

Hollywood was blindsided by *The Passion*. They saw the movie coming. They did not see the audience coming. Their lack of perception has revealed a blind spot in Hollywood. CNN, the cable TV news network, ran this report on its Web site. It appeared on January 15, 2004, less than six weeks before *The Passion* opened. If you want to understand Hollywood's mind-set, read it carefully.

> Even after the dust settles, a big question in Hollywood is: Who will see "The Passion"? Post-production continues, and the budget can be expected to increase by millions of dollars to cover print, distribution and advertising costs.
>
> Moreover, although Gibson agreed to have the dialogue subtitled, there's no guarantee there's a market for such a strongly religious film. Since the last successful wave of biblical epics in the 1950s, a number of films with biblical or spiritual themes have flopped at the box office, most recently Martin Scorsese's "The Last Temptation of Christ" (1988), Scorsese's "Kundun" (1997) and Michael Tolkin's strange "The Rapture" (1991).
>
> Taken together—the controversy, the religious theme, the subtitles—the outlook isn't very good, said one observer.
>
> "This film has all the makings of a [box-office] bomb," entertainment publicist Michael Levine told The Washington Times.[29]

Notice what their reference points were: Scorsese's *The Last Temptation of Christ*, Scorsese's *Kundun*, and Michael Tolkin's *The Rapture*. These were movies calculated to offend Christians, who are the mass market for religious films. As the popular phrase goes, Hollywood does not have a clue. Jesus described the industry well:

> Can the blind lead the blind? shall they not both fall into the ditch (Luke 6:39b)?

From the looks of the size of the pile-up on the Sunset Boulevard offramp of the Hollywood Freeway, the correct answer appears to be "yes."

Notes

1. Will and Ariel Durant, *Interpretations of Life: A Survey of Contemporary Literature* (New York: Simon and Schuster, 1970), ch. XVI.

2. Nikos Kazantzakis, *The Last Temptation of Christ* (New York: Scribners Paperback Fiction, [1960] 1998), p. 18.

3. *Ibid.*, p. 145.

4. *Ibid.*, p. 145.

5. *Ibid.*, p. 146.

6. *Ibid.*, p. 495.

7. *Ibid.*, p. 454.

8. *Ibid.*, p. 457.

9. *Ibid.*, p. 496.

10. *Ibid.*, p. 28.

11. *Ibid.*, p. 127.

12. *Ibid.*, p. 146.

13. *Ibid.*, p. 269.

14. *Ibid.*, p. 202.

15. *Ibid.*, p. 217.

16. *Ibid.*, p. 220.

17. *Ibid.*, p. 157.

18. *Ibid.*, p. 1.

19. *Ibid.*, p. 2.

20. *Ibid.*, p. 2.

21. *Ibid.*, p. 322.

22. Michael Medved, *Hollywood vs. America: Popular Culture and the War on Traditional Values* (New York: HarperCollins, 1992), p. 36.

23. *Ibid.*, p. 40.

24. *Ibid.*, p. 41.

25. *Ibid.*, p. 49.

26. *Ibid.*, p. 47.

27. *Ibid.*, pp. 47–48.

28. Kazantzakis, *Last Temptation*, pp. 229–30.

29. "Gibson's film 'Passion' inflames tempers" (Jan. 15, 2004). http://tinyurl.com/q3bv

9

Re-Conquest

And the eyes of them that see shall not be dim, and the ears of them that hear shall hearken. The heart also of the rash shall understand knowledge, and the tongue of the stammerers shall be ready to speak plainly. The vile person shall be no more called liberal, nor the churl said to be bountiful. For the vile person will speak villany, and his heart will work iniquity, to practise hypocrisy, and to utter error against the LORD, to make empty the soul of the hungry, and he will cause the drink of the thirsty to fail (Isaiah 32:3–6).

IT IS NOT good enough to criticize the churl. The churl must be replaced by the liberal—not the theological liberal or the political liberal, but the person who is liberal in spirit and generous to the poor (with his own money, not someone else's).

There is an old political slogan: "You can't beat something with nothing." It is not good enough to organize boycotts of evil movies. God-fearing people must produce God-honoring movies. Mel Gibson has shown us the way. His reward has been great so far. Now it is our turn. Each person in his own zone of responsibility is asked by God to do a version of what Mel Gibson did.

Christians have comprehensive responsibilities. Christ's redemption is not limited to souls. It extends to wherever sin reigns. This is the meaning of the Great Commission

> And Jesus came and spake unto them, saying, All power is given unto me in heaven and in earth. Go ye therefore, and teach all nations, baptizing them in the name of the Father, and of the Son, and of the Holy Ghost: Teaching them to observe all things whatsoever I have commanded you: and, lo, I am with you always, even unto the end of the world. Amen (Matthew 28:18–20).[1]

This ancient assignment includes the redemption of culture. The problem is, Christians have ignored culture for too long. That is, they have ignored the means of changing culture. They have subcultures of their own. These subcultures are under-funded, without influence in the prevailing culture, and easily captured by the spiritual enemies of Christ. In the eleventh century, Christians invented the university. The universities were all captured by humanists. Institution by institution, Christians have surrendered.

Defeat and Reconquest

In 711, Arabs warriors crossed the straits of Gibraltar and launched the conquest of Western Europe. They were beaten militarily at the Battle of Tours in 732. They retreated back across the Pyrenees mountains, where they already controlled Spain. From then until the Muslims' final expulsion by Spain in 1492, the Spanish engaged in the re-conquest. It took over 750 years. They were patient. They were also relentless. They would not accept submission as a permanent answer. (The word "Islam" means "submission.")

It need not take centuries for Christians to re-conquer the West from the humanists. Humanists today are visibly out of gas. They have controlled the main institutions of this civilization, and they have made a terrible mess of things. The educational institutions are declining. The TV networks are losing their audience. The governments all over the

West are facing bankruptcy. Modern music, from atonal symphonies to rap, is ugly, and most people know it. Modern art is ugly, and all but the self-deluded know it. Humanism exists increasingly on borrowed money and tax revenues. It is on life-support.

Hollywood cannot get people back into the theaters. Now its crucial source of profit, the DVD, is threatened by low-cost pirating. Anything digital can be copied perfectly, cheaply, and easily by anyone with a computer. Only self-government can prevent this from happening: "Thou shalt not steal." For a generation, Hollywood has done its best to ridicule the Ten Commandments. Now it faces the consequences. The moguls are panic-stricken, for good reason. The days of wine and roses are about to end.

Into this circle of fear marched Mel Gibson. He visibly beat the Hollywood Establishment to a pulp. The experts had predicted a disaster for his movie. It made a fortune. The Hollywood elite had tried to stop him. They failed. They revealed in full public view what hardly anyone had suspected: *they do not understand the American public.* They do not know on which side their bread is buttered. Furthermore, they do not care. They are contemptuous of traditional values.

We are not facing people with great wisdom. We are facing a visibly shaken group of self-appointed insiders who have seen a Catholic from Connecticut and a New Zealander using a Catholic's novels make the big money in 2004.

What Now?

As you have seen at the bottom of every page, there is a Web site aimed at people who have decided, "I've had enough." This Web site offers specific strategies for using rented movies and cheap video cameras to begin a counter-attack. It offers a recruiting strategy—call it evangelism—using DVDs of great classic movies to bring people into the churches. It also offers Web links to attacks on *The Passion* and the results: failure.

The site is free. It has two levels. The public pages are for those people who want to monitor what Hollywood and the media have done and are doing to corrupt an entire civilization. It reports on *The Passion* and Mel Gibson's efforts to follow up on his success. Then there is a members-only section for Christians who are ready to commit to a program of re-conquest. It provides specific plans and tools.

We must start somewhere. Standing on the sidelines and wringing our hands is no substitute for victory. A daily mantra of "woe are we" is not what Christ expects from His people.

Like the Spanish people in (say) 800, we may be facing an uphill battle. But our assigned task should be obvious to every serious Christian and is inescapable: *re-conquest*. We must start where we are: small. This is a familiar situation for God's people.

> Moreover the word of the LORD came unto me, saying, The hands of Zerubbabel have laid the foundation of this house; his hands shall also finish it; and thou shalt know that the LORD of hosts hath sent me unto you. For who hath despised the day of small things? for they shall rejoice, and shall see the plummet in the hand of Zerubbabel with those seven; they are the eyes of the LORD, which run to and fro through the whole earth (Zechariah 4:8-10).

But we may not be Spain in 800. We may be Spain in 1400. Technology is delivering enormous capabilities into the hands of little people. The pace of social change is speeding up, as Mikhail Gorbachev can tell you. The bigger they are (USSR), the harder they fall.

There is much to learn. There is much to do. There is a Web site where you can begin your efforts. There will be others like you for you to interact with. Now is not the time to retreat. Mel Gibson could have retreated, comfortable with a next egg of over $25 million. He put his money where his heart was.

What about you? If you are fed up, start here.

www.americanvision.org/gibsonwar

Notes

[1]Kenneth L. Gentry, *The Greatness of the Great Commission: The Christian Enterprise in a Fallen World* (Tyler, Texas: Institute for Christian Economics, 1990).

Conclusion

And he spake a parable unto them, Can the blind lead the blind? shall they not both fall into the ditch (Luke 6:39)?

For who hath known the mind of the Lord, that he may instruct him? But we have the mind of Christ (I Corinthians 2:16).

Here we have two principles of knowledge. First, a principle of perception: blind people do not perceive the road ahead. They risk falling into the ditch. Second, a principle of interpretation: a person needs the mind of Christ, meaning the true principles of interpretation. Every person needs both: accurate perceptions and accurate principles of interpretation. Jesus taught that covenant-breakers in principle possess neither, but covenant-keepers in principle possess both.

I say "in principle." This does not mean that covenant-breakers are incompetent. God gives covenant-breakers the ability to function in the world. They make their contributions in history, whether for both good or evil.[1] In many cases they are more skilled than covenant-keepers are. They may have higher IQ's. But, in the final analysis, they insist that the Bible is incorrect about God, man, law, causation, and time. They claim to have a superior understanding of these issues. They are incorrect. They are blind leaders who will lead their followers into an eternal ditch.

But will they also lead their followers into a ditch in history? This is another way of asking: Are their Bible-denying vision and their Bible-denying principles of interpretation far better suited to success in history than the Christians' Bible-affirming vision and Bible-affirming principles of interpretation? I hope that you answer "no." The correct answer is "no."

This leads us to the next question. What is it, in practice, that has led to the Bible-deniers' greater institutional and cultural success ever since approximately 1700? To put it in language more familiar to modern Americans, why have Christians spent the last three centuries riding in the back of humanism's bus? It started out as our bus. We have been paying for most of the gasoline and repairs. Why have we been stuck in the back? Why don't we ever get to take control of the steering wheel? Why do humanists get to pick both the destination and the route?

Because our forefathers surrendered control, voluntarily, three centuries ago. They said, "Here, you take the wheel. We're tired of all the responsibility. We get no respect." Today's Christians, as the lawfully adopted children of the God who created the universe, still flee responsibility. So, they still sit in the back of the bus. But some of them have begun to catch on to what is happening. The bus is heading toward a ditch.

The question now is this: How can Christians get back in the driver's seat?

Mel Gibson has shown us the way.

Mel Gibson's Triumph

Mel Gibson represents what can be done by Christians and therefore what should be done. He put his money where his heart was. But, more important than this, he put his skills where his heart was. Had he not possessed the skills, the movie would have been the flop that Hollywood insiders predicted it would be. Money talks. Competence talks louder. Courage talks loudest of all. Mel Gibson possessed all three when he decided to make *The Passion of the Christ*. Result: he now has a whole lot more money.

For decades, he paid his dues. He was not an onlooker. He was not a hired hand with a pretty face. He did his work, as assigned, but he kept his eyes open. He saw how his employers did what they did. Then he imitated them. He directed. He learned about film distribution. He waited. He bided his time. Then he took decisive action. I keep thinking of Jesus' words:

"Go, and do thou likewise" (Luke 10:37b).

It is not enough to go about our business as paid servants in the household of our enemies. We are morally obligated to work in order to become owners of our own households. We are to be patient in whatever role that God has assigned us, but we must be ready to accept liberty whenever it is offered. Why? Because we are bought with a price, exactly as *The Passion* reveals.

> Let every man abide in the same calling wherein he was called. Art thou called being a servant? care not for it: but if thou mayest be made free, use it rather. For he that is called in the Lord, being a servant, is the Lord's freeman: likewise also he that is called, being free, is Christ's servant. Ye are bought with a price; be not ye the servants of men. Brethren, let every man, wherein he is called, therein abide with God (II Corinthians 7:20–24).[2]

What Mel Gibson has done on a grand scale, other Christians can do on a small scale. They can do this, and therefore they must do this. They must do it on a small scale until they have the money, the skills, and the courage to do it on a grand scale. But without courage, neither money nor skills will suffice.

> The LORD thy God, he will go over before thee, and he will destroy these nations from before thee, and thou shalt possess them: and Joshua, he shall go over before thee, as the LORD hath said. And the LORD shall do unto them as he did to Sihon and to Og, kings of the Amorites, and unto the land of them, whom he destroyed. And the LORD shall give them up before your face, that ye may do unto them according unto all the commandments which I have commanded you. Be strong and of a good courage, fear not, nor be afraid of them: for the LORD thy God, he it is that doth go with thee; he will not fail thee, nor forsake thee. And Moses called unto Joshua, and said unto him in

the sight of all Israel, Be strong and of a good courage: for thou must
go with this people unto the land which the LORD hath sworn unto
their fathers to give them; and thou shalt cause them to inherit it. And
the LORD, he it is that doth go before thee; he will be with thee, he will
not fail thee, neither forsake thee: fear not, neither be dismayed. And
Moses wrote this law, and delivered it unto the priests the sons of Levi,
which bare the ark of the covenant of the LORD, and unto all the elders
of Israel (Deuteronomy 31:3–9).[3]

Where Should We Start?

We start with God's revelation, the Bible. We must imitate the Bere-
ans and search the Scriptures daily.

And the brethren immediately sent away Paul and Silas by night unto
Berea: who coming thither went into the synagogue of the Jews. These
were more noble than those in Thessalonica, in that they received the
word with all readiness of mind, and searched the scriptures daily,
whether those things were so (Acts 17:10–11).

We need to find out for ourselves what the Bible has to say about God,
man, law, causation, and history. Then we need to search the Scriptures
to learn the standards that apply to our own lives, including our paid
occupations and our unpaid service to others. We must become faithful
in small things until such time as we are sufficiently competent to accomplish larger things.

Think of Bob Jones, Sr. He started out as a salesman. Before he died,
he had established a college and had put together the finest collection of
European religious paintings in the world. Go, and do thou likewise.

God's people possess greater vision and greater favor in the eyes of
God than their enemies possess. If they are sitting in the back of the
bus, this is because they have not yet become sufficiently wealthy, sufficiently competent, and sufficiently courageous to buy the bus, fire the
driver, and let him and his friends sit in the back of the bus. It is not our
task to try to grab the wheel away from the driver and commandeer the

bus. If we adopt that strategy, we are more likely either to crash the bus or get thrown off.

Hollywood Is Running Scared

When the Israelite spies came into Jericho, Rahab told them that everyone in the land had been terrified of them for a generation.

> And she said unto the men, I know that the LORD hath given you the land, and that your terror is fallen upon us, and that all the inhabitants of the land faint because of you. For we have heard how the LORD dried up the water of the Red sea for you, when ye came out of Egypt; and what ye did unto the two kings of the Amorites, that were on the other side Jordan, Sihon and Og, whom ye utterly destroyed. And as soon as we had heard these things, our hearts did melt, neither did there remain any more courage in any man, because of you: for the LORD your God, he is God in heaven above, and in earth beneath (Joshua 2:9–11).

The people of Israel had wandered aimlessly in the wilderness for four decades, not suspecting that the giants in the land were afraid of them. The giants had looked so fearsome. They were in fact fearful.

Consider Hollywood. Hollywood is in disarray. Every time we go to the movies, we can see how fearful they are. The industry is running ads before each movie, ads that plead for people, meaning teenagers and young adults, not to download movies off the Internet. The moguls get studio technicians to front for them. These technicians tell the story of their craftsmanship, and then remind the viewers that it is wrong to steal. They are correct. It is wrong to steal. But where did the targeted audience learn otherwise?

We have here a fine example of biblical cause and effect in operation. Hollywood has spent forty years producing movies that celebrate the undermining of people's morality, and now the moguls have awakened to smell the digital coffee. They have aimed R-rated debauchery at teenage boys who take their girlfriends to the movies. They have deliberately produced films that arouse the girls sexually to make them more pliant. But then reality strikes: the fornicators have access to high speed phone lines. What the boys did to their girl friends last night, they are doing to Hollywood today. Surprise, surprise! The moguls cry out in horror: "But you said you'd still respect me in the morning!"

Attendance has stayed flat since 1965. Hollywood has bet the farm on film rentals. But now DVD technology and high speed Internet access have combined to allow file-sharing. There is nothing Hollywood can do about it. They threaten to sue violators, one by one, but the available statistics indicate that something in the range of 40 million Americans are downloading music without paying. They are soon going to do the same with movies. Every corporate distribution model in the entertainment industry has been blasted by digital buckshot.

They are terrified in Hollywood, as well they should be. Dr. Frankenstein has created a moral monster, and now the monster has invaded the archives, laptop in hand. There is a smile on his face. He is saying, over and over, "Movies . . . free . . . good!" He is not much for dialogue, but he is skilled with Windows' dialogue boxes. "Movies . . . free . . . good!"

It would not be right for Christians to take advantage of Hollywood's vulnerability to digital theft. Just because you have been handed a stolen key to the archives, you should not take "your fair share." Do not download an unpaid-for digital copy of *The Passion of the Christ*. Do not download any other movie or copyrighted performance. As Jesus said, "Therefore all things whatsoever ye would that men should do to you, do ye even so to them: for this is the law and the prophets" (Matthew 7:12). This is the famous golden rule, which is better known as "Do unto others as you would have others do unto you."[4] So, as the first step to establishing a Christian counter-offensive against Hollywood, take the following pledge:

> I hereby pledge before God that I will not download any movie from the Internet that is still protected by copyright law in my country, unless the movie is not being offered for sale by the copyright owner or unless the copyright owner has authorized such a download.

Then whenever you write a critical letter to a studio about some R-rated moral monstrosity that the studio has released, include a reference to the pledge. Let the letter-reader know that you are not a thief, but merely a ticket-buying customer who feels betrayed.

Hollywood deserves support from Christians in its campaign against copyright violations. But the fact is, the old copyright law is breaking down. It cannot be enforced economically. There is not enough money in Hollywood to enforce the old copyright laws in the courts. Hollywood must now rely on self-government by its customers. But Hollywood has spent four decades undermining the self-government of its paying customers. Hollywood has thumbed its nose at laws against pornography. Now its customers are thumbing their noses at copyright laws.

God is not mocked—not at zero price, anyway.

Beating Something with Something Better

There is an old political slogan: "You can't beat something with nothing." In every field of endeavor except one, Christians have been outclassed by humanists. The one area in which Christians have done better than anyone else is the creation of alphabets and dictionaries for tribal languages. Wycliffe Bible translators are the best in the world, and the humanistic linguists know it. In this one area, which is crucial to effective foreign missions, Christians have command of the field. When Christians see that they must do something well for the sake of the gospel, they can and do outperform their enemies, who are not equally motivated. But only in this one area of culture—applied linguistics—have Christians acknowledged that they have a moral obligation before God to be the best. In every other area, Christians have been in retreat, or worse. In most of these areas, Christians have voluntarily handed over the keys of the bus to the humanists and have told them, "You drive."

Christians suffer from an inferiority complex. They think they are inferior in things cultural. Yet they know that their God is superior. They know the words of Jesus, which they call the Great Commission.

And Jesus came and spake unto them, saying, All power is given unto me in heaven and in earth. Go ye therefore, and teach all nations, baptizing them in the name of the Father, and of the Son, and of the Holy Ghost: Teaching them to observe all things whatsoever I have commanded you: and, lo, I am with you always, even unto the end of the world. Amen (Matthew 28:18–20).

Only a handful of Christians remember the two verses that preceded this declaration. These two verses tell us a great deal about the reason for our present condition of inferior cultural status.

Then the eleven disciples went away into Galilee, into a mountain where Jesus had appointed them. And when they saw him, they worshipped him: but some doubted (Matthew 28:16–17).

Some of them doubted. Today, most Christians still doubt. They understand the magnitude of what the Great Commission requires of them. They do not believe that members of the church of Jesus Christ can ever come close to fulfilling Jesus' comprehensive requirement. They do not believe that Jesus' promise to the disciples on the night before His crucifixion was meaningful.

Nevertheless I tell you the truth; It is expedient for you that I go away: for if I go not away, the Comforter will not come unto you; but if I depart, I will send him unto you. And when he is come, he will reprove the world of sin, and of righteousness, and of judgment: Of sin, because they believe not on me; Of righteousness, because I go to my Father, and ye see me no more; Of judgment, because the prince of this world is judged (John 16:7–11).

They do not think that His ascension into heaven to sit at the right hand of God is relevant to the church's ability to fulfill the Great Commission.

Some of them feel so bad about this that they deny that the Great Commission really means what it says. They deny the greatness of the

Great Commission. It means souls-only evangelism, they say. Satan's agents lawfully own culture, they say. They are incorrect. The Great Commission is very great. It is comprehensive. It commands Christians to bring the gospel of redemption to every person. The gospel and the Holy Spirit together provide sufficient healing power to redeem every nook and cranny of God's creation.[5] Perfection is not possible in history because of sin, but cultural victory is possible. While we cannot meet God's perfect standards in history, we can do far better than God's enemies in approaching perfection as a limit.[6] Jesus is in heaven, and Satan is in hell. History's playing field is not level. It is tilted by God in favor of Christ's people.

Conclusion

We cannot beat something with nothing. We can beat something with something better. As Christians, we have something better: the law and the prophets. We also have the Holy Spirit, who empowers us to obey the law and the prophets. The resurrection is behind us. The ascension is behind us (Acts 1:9). The sending of the Holy Spirit is behind us (Acts 2:4). What more can we legitimately expect to be given? As the two men dressed in white told the disciples: "Ye men of Galilee, why stand ye gazing up into heaven" (Acts 1:11a)?

The same question applies to us. Mel Gibson has not stood around, gazing up into heaven. Neither should we.

Notes

1. Gary North, *Dominion and Common Grace: The Biblical Basis of Progress* (Tyler, Texas: Institute for Christian Economics, 1987). Available free at www.freebooks. com.

2. Gary North, *Judgment and Dominion: An Economic Commentary on First Corinthians*, electronic edition (West Fork, Arkansas: Institute for Christian Economics, 2001). Available free: www.demischools.org/corinthians.pdf.

3. Gary North, *Inheritance and Dominion: An Economic Commentary on Deuteronomy*, 2nd electronic edition (Harrisonburg, Virginia: Dominion Educational Ministries, Inc., [1999] 2003), ch. 73. Available free: www.demischools.org/deuteronomy-v3.pdf.

4. Gary North, *Priorities and Dominion: An Economic Commentary on Matthew*, 2nd electronic edition (Harrisonburg, Virginia: Dominion Educational Ministries, Inc., [2000] 2003), ch. 16. Available free: www.demischools.org/matthew.pdf.

5. Kenneth L. Gentry, Jr., *The Greatness of the Great Commission: The Christian Enterprise in a Fallen World* (Tyler, Texas: Institute for Christian Economics, 1990). Available free on www.freebooks.com.

6. Kenneth L. Gentry, Jr., *He Shall Have Dominion: A Postmillennial Eschatology*, 2nd ed. (Tyler, Texas: Institute for Christian Economics, 1997). Available free on www.freebooks.com.

Scripture Index

Subject Index